GUERNICA
and
Other Plays

D1055922

GUERNICA
and
Other Plays

BY ARRABAL

translated from the French
by Barbara Wright

GROVE PRESS, INC., NEW YORK

These translations copyright ©1967 by Calder & Boyars Ltd.,
London
All Rights Reserved
Guernica, The Labyrinth, The Tricycle, and *Picnic on the Battlefield*
were originally published in *Théâtre,* copyright ©1961 by René
Julliard, éditeur, Paris, France

Library of Congress Catalog Card Number: 79-84570
First Evergreen Edition, 1969
First Printing

CAUTION: These plays are fully protected, in whole, in part, or in
any form under the copyright laws of the United States of America,
the British Empire including the Dominion of Canada, and all
other countries of the Copyright Union, and are subject to royalty.
All rights, including professional, amateur, motion picture, radio,
television, recitation, public reading, and any method of
photographic reproduction, are strictly reserved. For professional
and amateur rights in Great Britain all inquiries should be addressed
to Margaret Ramsay Ltd., 14a Goodwin's Court, London W.C.2,
England; for American rights, all inquiries should be addressed to
Ninon Tallon Karlweis, 250 East 65th Street, New York, N.Y. 10021

Manufactured in the United States of America

CONTENTS

GUERNICA

The tree of liberty in Guernica escaped
the massacre of the town, and still stands.

CHARACTERS

FANCHOU   *An old Basque man*
LIRA   *An old Basque woman*

Also taking part in the play:

A Woman and her 10 year old daughter
A Journalist
A Writer
An Officer

Guernica *was performed in German by the Schloss-theater company at Celle, which presented the play in Paris in June 1961 at the Théâtre du Vieux-Colombier.*

GUERNICA

*The sound of the boots of marching troops is heard for
some ten seconds. Then the sound of an air raid: aeroplanes and exploding bombs. The curtain rises when the
raid is over. The interior of a bombed house: crumbling
walls, debris, stones.* FANCHOU *is in the house, near a
table, in despair.*

FANCHOU: My precious, my lamb.
He searches a pile of rubble on his right, unsuccessfully.
Where are you, my lamb?
He goes on searching.
LIRA'S VOICE [*plaintively*]: Darling.
FANCHOU: Have you finished peeing?
LIRA'S VOICE: I can't get out. I'm stuck. Everything's
collapsed.
FANCHOU *climbs on to the table with some difficulty,
trying to see* LIRA. *He raises himself on tiptoe. He sees
her, and looks pleased.*
FANCHOU: Look at me.
He stands on tiptoe again.
LIRA'S VOICE: Are you there?
FANCHOU: Go carefully, my precious.
LIRA'S VOICE: Ow, ouch.
She moans like a child.
FANCHOU: Have you hurt yourself?
Pause. FANCHOU *looks anxious.*
LIRA'S VOICE [*plaintively*]: Yes. All the stones fell on top of
me.
FANCHOU: Try and stand up.
LIRA'S VOICE: There's no point, I won't be able to get out.
FANCHOU: Make an effort.

9

LIRA'S VOICE: Tell me you still love me.

FANCHOU: Of course, you know I do. [*Pause.*] You'll see, when you get out we'll do all sorts of lovely dirty things.

LIRA'S VOICE: Of course we will. [*Sounding pleased.*] You'll never change.

> *Sound of aeroplanes. Bombs start falling again for a few seconds. The raid stops.*

FANCHOU: Have any more stones fallen on you?

LIRA'S VOICE: No. Have they on you, my precious?

FANCHOU: No. Make an effort and get out of there.

LIRA'S VOICE: I can't. [*Pause.*] Look and see if they've hit the tree.

> FANCHOU *gets down off the table with difficulty. He goes over to the left. He has to clear a lot of rubble out of the way. Part of the window appears.* FANCHOU *looks out of it. He seems pleased. He comes back. He climbs on to the·table again.*

FANCHOU: No, they haven't hit it, it's still there.

> *Pause.*

LIRA'S VOICE [*plaintively*]: What am I going to do?

FANCHOU: Try and stand up carefully, very carefully.

LIRA'S VOICE: I can't.

FANCHOU: Make an effort.

LIRA'S VOICE: I'll try.

FANCHOU [*speaking slowly*]: Carefully does it, that's right, very carefully.

> *There is a sound of falling rubble. Plaintive moans from* LIRA.

Have you hurt yourself? [*Silence.*] What's happening? Say something. Have you hurt yourself?

> *Plaintive moans from* LIRA.

Have you really hurt yourself?

LIRA'S VOICE [*sadly*]: Yes. [*She whimpers like a child.*] Some stones fell on my arm; it's bleeding.

FANCHOU: Bleeding?

LIRA'S VOICE: Yes.

FANCHOU: A lot?

LIRA'S VOICE: Yes, a lot.

FANCHOU: Is it a scratch or a wound?

LIRA'S VOICE: It's a scratch, but there's a lot of blood.

FANCHOU: I'll go and get you some cotton wool.

> FANCHOU *searches the rubble. He shifts some of the debris, but more and more rubble falls. He gives up. He goes back and gets up on the table again.*

The wardrobe's buried in rubble.

> LIRA *whimpers like a child.*

Don't cry. Put a bit of saliva on your arm and tie your handkerchief round it.

> LIRA *groans. Enter right, the* JOURNALIST *and the WRITER. The* JOURNALIST *has a notebook in his hand. The* WRITER *walks round* FANCHOU *inquisitively and examines him carefully. He suddenly stops for a moment in the middle of the stage.*

WRITER [*to the* JOURNALIST]: And you can say, too that I'm writing a novel, and perhaps a film, on the Spanish civil war.

> *The* WRITER *and the* JOURNALIST *walk towards the left.*

WRITER [*confidently*]: This heroic and paradoxical people, which reflects the spirit of Lorca's poems, Goya's paintings, and Buñuel's films, is demonstrating, in this dreadful war, its courage, its capacity for suffering, its . . .

> *The* WRITER *and the* JOURNALIST *go out, left. The* WRITER's *voice fades away in the distance.*

FANCHOU: Do you feel any better?

LIRA'S VOICE: A bit. [*Pause. Plaintive voice.*] But not much.

FANCHOU: Would you like me to tell you a nice story so it doesn't hurt any more?

LIRA'S VOICE: You're no good at telling stories.

FANCHOU: Would you like me to tell you the one about the woman who was in the lavatory and who got buried in the rubble? [*Pause.*] Don't you like that one?

LIRA'S VOICE: It hurts a lot.

FANCHOU: It'll soon be better, you'll see. I'll act the clown and make you laugh.

> FANCHOU *does an awkward dance and pulls all kinds of faces. Then he bursts out laughing.*

11

FANCHOU: Did you like it?

LIRA'S VOICE: I can't see you.

> *Sound of aeroplanes. Raid. While this is going on a woman and her little girl cross the stage from right to left, looking angry and helpless (see the Picasso painting). The raid ends.*

FANCHOU: Are you all right, my lamb?

> *Long pause.*

LIRA'S VOICE: Darling, I feel terrible. I'm going to die.

FANCHOU: You're going to die? [*Pause.*] Are you really and truly going to die? D'you want me to tell the family?

LIRA'S VOICE [*irritable*]: What d'you mean, the family?

FANCHOU: Isn't that what people say?

LIRA'S VOICE: What a rotten memory you've got. Don't you remember we haven't got a family any more?

FANCHOU: Hm! Nor we have! [*He cogitates.*] What about Joséchou?

LIRA'S VOICE: You must be dreaming! Have you really forgotten that he was shot at Burgos?

FANCHOU: Well you can't say it was my fault. I always told you I didn't want a boy. Whenever a war crops up they get killed. Whereas if we'd had a girl the house would be nice and tidy now.

LIRA'S VOICE: That's it, nothing but reproaches. It wasn't my fault.

FANCHOU: Don't be cross, my love, I didn't mean to hurt your feelings.

LIRA'S VOICE: You're never a bit sorry for me.

FANCHOU: Oh yes I am. When you get out of there I'll give you another one, if you like, just to show that I don't hold it against you.

LIRA'S VOICE: But you can't any more.

FANCHOU: That's right, now tell me I'm not a man any more, go on.

LIRA'S VOICE: No, it's not that, it's just that you can't get an erection any more.

FANCHOU: I can't, can't I? Well, you're the only one who says that. Don't you remember that Saturday?

12

LIRA'S VOICE: Which Saturday?

FANCHOU: Which Saturday d'you think? You'll tell me you've forgotten that, next.

LIRA'S VOICE: Are you going to start boasting all over again?

FANCHOU: I'm not boasting. It's just the plain, honest truth, but you don't want to admit it. [*Pause.*]

LIRA'S VOICE: Have another look and see if they've got the tree.

> FANCHOU *gets off the table. He goes over to the window. He opens it. An* OFFICER *appears on the other side of it. They look at each other very gravely for quite some time.* FANCHOU *hangs his head apprehensively. The* OFFICER *laughs mirthlessly and plays with a pair of handcuffs he is holding.* FANCHOU, *still hanging his head, shuts the window. He comes back looking terrified. He gets up on the table.*

Well?

> *Pause.*

Well? Is it still there?

FANCHOU: I don't know.

LIRA'S VOICE: What d'you mean, you don't know?

FANCHOU: I couldn't see it.

LIRA'S VOICE [*plaintively*]: That's fine—here I am, stuck, all I ask you to do is look and see if they've hit the tree and you won't even do that.

FANCHOU: I couldn't.

LIRA'S VOICE [*plaintively*]: All right, have it your own way.

> FANCHOU *gets down from the table. Fearfully, he goes over to the window. He opens it anxiously. He looks out of it. He goes back to the table and climbs on to it. He raises himself up on tiptoe, looking pleased.*

FANCHOU: It's still there.

LIRA'S VOICE [*proudly*]: I told you it would be. [*Pause. Very sadly.*] Help me a bit, though. Don't leave me all by myself.

FANCHOU: What d'you want me to do?

LIRA'S VOICE [*plaintively*]: Can't you think of anything? How

13

you've changed. It's quite obvious that you don't love me any more.

FANCHOU: But I do, my lamb. Try and stand up. Stretch your arm out, I'll try and reach it.

> FANCHOU *raises himself as high as he can and stretches out his arm towards the rubble. While* FANCHOU *is trying to grasp* LIRA's *hand, the* OFFICER *enters, right. The* OFFICER *looks at* FANCHOU, *who has his back to him.*

Make an effort. If you can stretch just a little bit further I'll be able to reach you. A bit more. There. There.

> FANCHOU *is on tiptoe. The* OFFICER *pushes him from behind and makes him fall over. The* OFFICER *immediately goes out, right.* FANCHOU *laboriously gets up again. He looks towards the right. The* OFFICER *appears at the window. He laughs mirthlessly and plays with his handcuffs.* FANCHOU *looks at the window apprehensively. When their eyes meet the* OFFICER *stops laughing and playing with the handcuffs. They look at each other gravely.* FANCHOU *hangs his head. The* OFFICER *again starts laughing mirthlessly and playing with the handcuffs. He finally disappears.* FANCHOU *raises his head and looks over towards the window; he seems relieved.*

LIRA'S VOICE: Ow, ouch, why've you gone and left me?

FANCHOU: I slipped. Have you hurt yourself, my lamb?

LIRA'S VOICE: Some more stones have fallen on me. Ouch.

FANCHOU: I'm sorry.

LIRA'S VOICE: I can't rely on you.

FANCHOU: Oh yes you can. I've got a surprise for you: a present.

> FANCHOU *takes a piece of string and a flabby object out of his pocket. He inflates it with his mouth. It's a blue balloon. He ties it with the string. He attaches a stone to the end of the string.*

[*Very pleased*]:Catch this stone I'm throwing over. [*He throws it over the wall.*] Have you got it?

LIRA'S VOICE: Yes.

FANCHOU: Pull the string.

LIRA *does so. The balloon settles over her head.*
Look up in the air. Can you see it?

Sound of aeroplanes. Raid. A deafening row. While it is going on the woman and the little girl cross from right to left. They are pushing a wheelbarrow. On it is a packing case on which the word DINAMITA *is written. They look angry and helpless. The raid ends.*
My lamb! [*Pause. Worried.*] My lamb!

The balloon moves up and down.
Are you all right?

The balloon moves up and down.
Say something.

Long silence.
Won't you say something to me? Are you cross with me? It's not my fault. [*Pause.*] Now if only *I* had a hand in things. [*Pause.*] *I* didn't destroy the houses. [*Pleased.*] In any case, they haven't got the tree. [*Suddenly.*] Are you going to be cross for ever and ever? [*Silence.*] Are you mortally offended? [*Silence.*] So that's the way you love me. All right. Have it your own way. [*He looks the other way, obstinately, as if he doesn't care. He crosses his arms.*] You heard me, I suppose? Have it your own way, it's all the same to me. [*Pause.*] And don't turn round afterwards and tell me that I started it and that I'm so difficult. This time it's obvious; I haven't done a thing, you're the one that's refusing to talk. I saw what you were up to— you started by saying that I couldn't make it, that Saturday, and now you refuse to talk to me. [*Pause.*] Don't you even want to play with the balloon?

FANCHOU *turns round to have a look. The balloon is moving gently up and down.*
Ah! Her ladyship can't talk, she's tired, she only deigns to play with the balloon. Right—two can play at that game. [*Pause.*] But say something, tell me what you want, even if it's something horrid, but say something. [*Long silence.*] Oh, very well.

Once again he adopts a sulky look. He crosses his arms and looks in the opposite direction. Enter, right, the

15

WRITER *and the* JOURNALIST, *still holding his notebook.*
FANCHOU *is terrified, and takes refuge under the table.*
The WRITER *smells him out. He examines him from every*
angle and prevents him from moving.

WRITER [*to the* JOURNALIST]: What a complex, heart-rending
people! Put that down—no, say that the complexity of
this heart-rending people flourishes in a spontaneous
fashion in this cruel and fratricidal war. [*Pleased with*
himself.] Not bad, eh? [*He hesitates.*] No, no, leave out
that sentence. Too emphatic; I must find something more
definitive, more restrained. [*He considers.*] It'll come,
it'll come.

FANCHOU *is still lying on the ground, under the table,*
terrified. The WRITER *and the* JOURNALIST *go out, left.*
The WRITER'S *voice fades away in the distance.*

WRITER'S VOICE: What a novel I shall make out of all this.
What a novel! Or a play, perhaps, and even a film. And
what a film!

LIRA'S VOICE: Who were you talking to?

FANCHOU: Her ladyship has found her tongue. She's not
dumb any more. Well, I may as well tell you that now it's
my turn to refuse to talk.

LIRA'S VOICE: [*plaintively*]: Darling, it hurts, it hurts terribly.
You aren't a bit sorry for me.

FANCHOU [*anxiously*]: What's the matter—are you ill?

LIRA'S VOICE: Can't you see I'm covered in stones and I
can't move.

FANCHOU: I wasn't thinking about it.

LIRA'S VOICE: You never do think about me.

FANCHOU: Nor I do. I ought to tie a knot in my handkerchief.

LIRA'S VOICE: What would become of you without me?
You're so irresponsible.

FANCHOU [*angry and boastful*]: That's what you always say.
Right then, I'll marry someone else. I can still turn
people's heads, you know. You ought to see the way the
baker's wife looks at me when I go and fetch the bread
every morning.

LIRA'S VOICE: That's fine. So you deceive me with the first

performing dog you meet, now. I knew I couldn't trust you.

FANCHOU: *She* looks at *me*. I just ignore her.

LIRA'S VOICE: That's what *you* say. I'd like to see you.

FANCHOU: I haven't done anything, I swear.

LIRA'S VOICE: More of your drunkard's oaths. You always promised you'd take me away on a honeymoon.

FANCHOU: I haven't forgotten. The moment the war's over we'll go for a holiday. I'll take you to Paris.

LIRA'S VOICE: Huh yes, Paris. You want to have a good time.

FANCHOU: You see the way you are: you never agree with me.

LIRA'S VOICE [*plaintively*]: Ouch. Some more stones are falling on me.

FANCHOU [*worried*]: Did they hurt a lot? [LIRA *groans*.] Oh dear, this war business is really very annoying.

LIRA'S VOICE: Do something for me.

FANCHOU: What shall I do?

LIRA'S VOICE: Get a doctor.

FANCHOU: They've sent them all away.

LIRA'S VOICE: You might as well say straight out that you don't want to do anything to help me.

FANCHOU: But you don't seem to realise that there's a war on.

LIRA'S VOICE: We haven't done anyone any harm.

FANCHOU: That doesn't count. The next thing you'll be saying is that I'm the one who forgets everything. You've already forgotten how these things are.

LIRA'S VOICE: They might at least make an exception for us; we're old.

FANCHOU: What *are* you thinking of? War is a serious business. It's quite obvious you never had any education.

LIRA'S VOICE: That's right, now you're going to insult me. You might as well say straight out that you don't love me.

FANCHOU [*tenderly*]: I didn't mean to hurt you, my love.

LIRA'S VOICE: You didn't mean to hurt me, but you did.

17

How you've changed! In the old days, nothing was too good for me.

FANCHOU: It's just the same now.

LIRA'S VOICE: And this business of education. Don't you think I've got feelings too?

FANCHOU: But I said it just like that, without thinking.

LIRA'S VOICE: Take it back.

FANCHOU: I take it back.

LIRA'S VOICE: No mental reservations?

FANCHOU: No, I swear.

LIRA'S VOICE: What on?

FANCHOU: Same as usual.

LIRA'S VOICE: Right. I hope you aren't going to start all over again.

Pause.

FANCHOU: Can't you stand up, and try and get out of there?

LIRA'S VOICE: But whenever I move, stones start falling.

FANCHOU: We must do something.

Sound of aeroplanes. Raid. While it is going on the mother and daughter cross from right to left. The mother is carrying some sporting guns. The daughter has three. LIRA's balloon bursts. The raid ends.

LIRA'S VOICE [*plaintively*]: They've busted my balloon.

FANCHOU: The brutes! They shoot just anyhow, without aiming.

LIRA'S VOICE: They did it on purpose.

FANCHOU: No, but they shoot without aiming, they don't bother.

LIRA'S VOICE: The brutes! First they demolish our house and then, to crown it all, they bust our balloon.

FANCHOU: They're impossible.

LIRA'S VOICE: See if they've hit the tree.

FANCHOU gets down off the table. He goes over to the window. The OFFICER appears on the other side of it. The OFFICER looks gravely at FANCHOU. FANCHOU is terrified and hangs his head. The OFFICER laughs mirthlessly and plays with the handcuffs with one finger. The OFFICER

18

disappears from the window. FANCHOU *raises his head. He can't see anyone. He puts his head cautiously out of the window. He looks at the tree. He seems pleased. Laughter behind him, to his right. He turns round to the right. The* OFFICER'S *sneering face appears, and then immediately disappears.* FANCHOU *is frightened and doesn't know what to do. Laughter to his left. He turns round. The* OFFICER'S *sneering face appears on his left. It immediately disappears.* FANCHOU *is frightened and doesn't know where to look. Laughter on his left, then on his right, then left, then right, then left, then right.* FANCHOU *is terrified and doesn't budge. The* OFFICER *enters, right. Looking serious and observant. He seems very much concerned with* FANCHOU. *He pulls a sandwich out of his pocket, and starts gnawing at the bread, all the time keeping his eyes glued on him. He goes over and stands near* FANCHOU. FANCHOU *retreats. The* OFFICER *moves again and stands right by him.* FANCHOU *timidly tries to escape. The* OFFICER *sticks to him, doesn't take his eyes off him, and finally drives him into a corner.* FANCHOU *can't move, now. He keeps his eyes fixed on the ground. The* OFFICER *extends his elbows and bars the way to him. The* OFFICER *goes on calmly gnawing at his bread and doesn't take his eyes off him.*
Long silence.

LIRA'S VOICE: What on earth are you doing?

FANCHOU *can't move, and doesn't answer.*

That's right, now you're going to leave me alone.

The OFFICER *munches his sandwich impassively, still keeping* FANCHOU *a prisoner.*

[*Tenderly.*] Come on, my love.

The OFFICER *stops eating and grimaces: he bares all his teeth and looks as if he is laughing, but makes no sound.* FANCHOU *looks sheepish and hangs his head even lower. Then the* OFFICER *stops laughing and starts eating again.*

Are you angry? [*Pause.*] All right then—it *is* true that you could, that Saturday. [*Pause.*] Now are you satisfied?

The OFFICER *stops eating and grimaces. He bares all his*

19

teeth and looks as if he is laughing, but makes no sound.
FANCHOU *looks sheepish and hangs his head even lower.*
Then the OFFICER *stops laughing and starts eating again.*
I do realise that you're a great success with the ladies—
and specially with the baker's wife.

> *Same business. Then the* OFFICER *carefully disposes of*
> *the remains of the sandwich: he wraps it up in newspaper.*
> *He wipes his mouth meticulously with the sleeves of*
> FANCHOU'S *jacket. He polishes his boots with the bottom*
> *of* FANCHOU'S *jacket. Then he turns round and goes off,*
> *right, looking very martial.* FANCHOU *laughs merrily and*
> *puts out his tongue. Then he quickly checks himself, and*
> *looks terrified. He looks all around him. He makes sure*
> *that no one can see him. He puts out his tongue and makes*
> *a long nose several times. He laughs merrily and climbs*
> *back on to the table.*

FANCHOU: The tree's still there, my lamb.

LIRA'S VOICE: Did it take you all this time to find *that* out?

FANCHOU: I like to do things properly.

LIRA'S VOICE: You haven't been to see the baker's wife, by any chance?

FANCHOU: Who d'you take me for? Do you think I'd go having affairs in the middle of a war?

> *Air raid. Aeroplanes, bombs. During which the woman*
> *and her daughter cross the stage from right to left,*
> *pushing a pram piled high with cartridges. The raid ends.*
> *Long silence.*

My own Lira!

> *Long silence.*

LIRA'S VOICE: What?

FANCHOU: Why didn't you ever have lovers?

LIRA'S VOICE: Lovers? [*A short laugh.*]

FANCHOU: Yes, lovers. [*He laughs. Then he stops.*]

LIRA'S VOICE: *Me*? [*A short laugh.*]

FANCHOU: Yes, you.

LIRA'S VOICE: I never thought of it.

FANCHOU: You never think about *me*. I could have played

tricks on them. [*Pause.*] You ought to have had a least one. [*He considers the matter.*] A colonel.

LIRA'S VOICE: Oh yes, a colonel, that's the way you love me.

FANCHOU: You're always behind the times.

LIRA'S VOICE: Go on, insult me, as well.

FANCHOU: No, my lamb. [*Pause. Obstinately.*] But every self-respecting woman has lovers. [*Pause.*] You never wanted to do anything to help me: when I undress you so that my friends can touch you you always make a fuss.

LIRA'S VOICE: Because I catch a cold.

FANCHOU: You find excuses for everything you do.

LIRA'S VOICE: And you never think about anyone but yourself: you're an egoist.

FANCHOU: But I do it for *you.* [*He seems pleased with himself—he's had a good idea.*] You'll be able to write your autobiography later on.

LIRA'S VOICE: Ow! [*Pause.*] The stones are falling on me again. [*She groans.*] I'll never be able to move my feet again.

FANCHOU: Make an effort.

LIRA'S VOICE [*plaintively*]: They're buried!

FANCHOU: Things really are going from bad to worse.

LIRA'S VOICE: Is that all you can think of to say? You never worry about me.

FANCHOU: Yes I do, I'm worrying now. [*Suddenly.*] Do you want me to cry?

LIRA'S VOICE: I know what you're up to: you're going to play another trick of me.

FANCHOU: No I'm not—you'll see; I can really cry properly when I want to.

LIRA'S VOICE: I know *you.* It'd be all the same to you if I died.

FANCHOU: That's what *you* say. When you're dead I'll . . . [*He considers.*] I'll sleep with you three times running.

LIRA'S VOICE: Still bragging.

FANCHOU: Don't say you've already forgotten . . .

LIRA'S VOICE [*interrupting him indignantly*]: Oh yes, *I* know: that famous Saturday when . . .

FANCHOU [*angry*]: Next thing'll be that you'll be saying that *I'm* the one that's nasty to *you*.
More stones fall.
LIRA'S VOICE: Ow, ow. [*Her groans increase.*] I really am going to die.
FANCHOU: Shall I get a priest?
LIRA'S VOICE: What d'you mean, a priest?
FANCHOU: Isn't that what people say?
LIRA'S VOICE: What a rotten memory you've got: Don't you remember we aren't religious any more?
FANCHOU [*terrified*]: Who? Us?
LIRA'S VOICE: But you were the one who decided. Don't you remember?
FANCHOU [*who doesn't remember anything*]: Ah yes!
LIRA'S VOICE: You said that then we'd be . . . [*Pause. Emphatically.*] more mature.
FANCHOU [*surprised*]: Mature? Us?
LIRA'S VOICE: Of course.
FANCHOU: Now we're in a fine mess: you're going to die and you'll go to hell.
LIRA'S VOICE: For ever and ever?
FANCHOU: Naturally, for ever and ever. And the tortures! You'll see some fine ones. He does things properly, he does.
LIRA'S VOICE: Who d'you mean, he?
FANCHOU: Well, God.
LIRA'S VOICE: God?
A short laugh.
FANCHOU: Yes, God.
A short laugh.
They both laugh nervously in chorus.
Air raid. The sound of aeroplanes and bombs falling, during which the woman and her little girl cross from right to left. On her back the woman is carrying a bag full of makeshift ammunition. The child helps her as best she can. The raid ends.
LIRA'S VOICE: Ow, ow.
FANCHOU: What's happened?

LIRA'S VOICE: I'll never get out of here, now.

FANCHOU: Don't give up hope.

LIRA'S VOICE: The stones are up to my waist.

FANCHOU: Don't worry. You'll see, I'll find some way of getting you out.

LIRA'S VOICE: We really don't have any luck.

FANCHOU: It's all your fault, you and your passion for reading in the lavatory. You spend hours and hours there. What's happened to you doesn't surprise me in the least.

LIRA'S VOICE: Everything's always my fault.

FANCHOU: Don't take it like that, I didn't mean to hurt you. *Silence.*

LIRA'S VOICE: Why've they demolished the house?

FANCHOU: You have to be told the same thing over and over. [*Sounding each syllable separately.*] They're trying out high explosives and incendiary bombs. Next thing you'll be saying that I'm the one that forgets things.

LIRA'S VOICE: Couldn't they try them out somewhere else?

FANCHOU: You seem to think everything's so easy. They had to try them out on a town, after all.

LIRA'S VOICE: Why?

FANCHOU: You'll say that I'm making fun of you again, but it's quite obvious that you've never had the slightest bit of education. Why! Why! Why d'you think, except to find out whether they work.

LIRA'S VOICE: And then what?

FANCHOU: And then what? And then what? You're being stupid on purpose: if a bomb kills a lot of people, then it's a good bomb and they make some more, but if it doesn't kill anyone, it's no good and they don't make any more.

LIRA'S VOICE: Oh!

FANCHOU: You have to have everything explained to you.

LIRA'S VOICE [*annoyed*]: I don't see why you have to talk like that. I know very well I didn't have as much schooling as you did.

FANCHOU [*swollen with pride*]: I know everything, eh? People really might think I'd been to a university.

23

[*Pause. He looks pleased with himself. He's had a good idea.*] Anyone might take me for a professor, don't you think?

LIRA'S VOICE [*bored and sceptical*]: Yes, of course.

FANCHOU: In which case you'd be a professor's wife. And when people saw us in the street, they'd say: 'look at the professors.' [*Pause.*] We'd be one up on them. We'd have visiting cards and we'd go to conferences. All I need is the umbrella. And anyway, you're pretty well educated, with all you've read in the lavatory!

LIRA'S VOICE: Are you starting all over again?

FANCHOU: Don't you agree?

LIRA'S VOICE: Us? Professors?

FANCHOU: You never agree with my ideas. It's always been the same. If you're going to start again, right, I'm off for good. [*Irritated.*] I don't want you to live with a man who talks nonsense. Goodbye!

FANCHOU *crouches down and makes a noise on the table so that it sounds as if he's going away.*

LIRA'S VOICE: Darling! Are you going to leave me all alone?

LIRA *groans.* FANCHOU *doesn't move. He's still squatting.* Come back, darling!

Long silence. FANCHOU *doesn't move, he's still squatting.* But it was just a joke. [*Pause.*] You know very well how much I admire you. [*Long pause.*] You'd make a magnificent professor. [*Pause.*] When people hear you talk they take you for a captain, or even an antique dealer.

Long silence. FANCHOU *looks proud.* Darling! [*Pause.*] Are you going to leave me all alone? [*Pause.*] Come over here!

Long pause. Same business.

LIRA'S VOICE: Ow, ow. [*She weeps.*] The stones have started falling again.

FANCHOU [*standing up, anxious*]: What's happening, my angel? Have you hurt yourself?

LIRA'S VOICE: I'll soon be completely buried. And that's the moment you choose to leave me. You're just heartless.

FANCHOU: Well, you started it.

LIRA'S VOICE: It was just a joke.

FANCHOU: Swear you won't do it any more.

LIRA'S VOICE: I swear.

FANCHOU: What on?

LIRA'S VOICE: The usual.

FANCHOU: No mental reservations?

LIRA'S VOICE: No mental reservations.

FANCHOU: Right. I hope you won't start again.

> *Air raid. Sound of bombs and aeroplanes, during which the woman and her daughter cross from right to left pulling a little handcart full of old rifles. The raid ends.*

LIRA'S VOICE: Ow, ow. Now I can't move my arms.

FANCHOU: Don't worry, I'll get you out.

LIRA'S VOICE: But the stones are up to my neck.

FANCHOU: Don't worry. You'll see, I'll think of something.

LIRA'S VOICE: I'm going to die.

FANCHOU: Do you want me to get a lawyer for your will?

LIRA'S VOICE: What d'you mean, my will?

FANCHOU: Isn't that what people say?

LIRA'S VOICE: Are you going to start all over again?

FANCHOU [*flattered*]: You ought to make one. I'd show it to the neighbours.

LIRA'S VOICE: All you ever think of is showing off.

FANCHOU: But I'm doing it for you. That's what all great ladies do. You ought to be making your will and thinking up your last words.

LIRA'S VOICE: What d'you mean . . . my last words?

FANCHOU: The ones people say before they die. D'you want me to prompt you? You could say something about . . . [*He thinks, and then says quickly.*] life, or humanity . . .

LIRA'S VOICE [*interrupting him*]: Stop it, you're talking nonsense.

FANCHOU: D'you call that nonsense? Well you *are* frivolous!

LIRA'S VOICE [*plaintively*]: Are you going to start insulting me again?

25

FANCHOU: No, my little lamb.

LIRA'S VOICE: I can't move at all now. [*Plaintively*.] But when is this war going to be over?

FANCHOU: That's right, now her ladyship wants the war to be over when it suits *her* convenience.

LIRA'S VOICE [*whimpering*]: Can't they stop it?

FANCHOU: Of course they can't. The general said he wouldn't stop until he's occupied the whole country.

LIRA'S VOICE: All of it?

FANCHOU: Yes, of course, all of it.

LIRA'S VOICE: That's going a bit far.

FANCHOU: Generals don't do things by halves: it's all or nothing.

LIRA'S VOICE: What about the people?

FANCHOU: The people don't know anything about making wars. And in any case, the general is getting an awful lot of help.

LIRA'S VOICE: Then it's not a game any more!

FANCHOU: You don't suppose the general cares, do you?

LIRA'S VOICE: I can't move at all, now. If any more stones start falling I shall be completely buried.

FANCHOU: What a bore. Don't worry. You'll see, the raids will soon be over.

LIRA'S VOICE: For good?

FANCHOU: For good.

LIRA'S VOICE: How d'you know?

FANCHOU [*cut to the quick*]: Do you doubt my word?

LIRA'S VOICE: No. [*Sceptically*.] Why d'you suppose I should doubt it?

Three shells explode. A ghastly noise.

[*Weeping bitterly*.] Darling, I'm completely buried, come and rescue me.

FANCHOU: I'm coming this minute, my little lamb. You'll see, I'll get you out.

FANCHOU *goes over and climbs laboriously on to the debris.* LIRA *weeps.*

LIRA'S VOICE: This time I really am going to die.

FANCHOU: Don't panic. I'm coming.

FANCHOU *moves laboriously over the debris. He reaches the place where* LIRA *is.*

My little lamb. Here I am. Give me your hand.

LIRA'S VOICE: Can't you see I'm covered in stones?

FANCHOU: I'll get you free this minute. You just wait, I'll get you out.

Long raid. More stones fall. FANCHOU *too is buried under the rubble.*

As the long raid is just coming to an end, the woman crosses from right to left. The little girl isn't with her this time. She is carrying a small coffin on her shoulder. She looks angry and helpless (see the Picasso painting). She disappears, left.

In the background: the tree of liberty can be seen above the debris of the walls. The raid is over: there is now nothing but debris on the stage. Long silence.

Two coloured balloons float gently upwards from the exact spot where FANCHOU *and* LIRA *disappeared. Enter the* OFFICER, *who fires at them with his Lewis gun but doesn't hit them. The balloons disappear into the sky. The* OFFICER *fires again. From above,* FANCHOU *and* LIRA *can be heard laughing happily. The* OFFICER *is terrified, looks all round him, and goes out, right, quickly. Enter the* WRITER. *He gets up on to the table. He examines the place where* FANCHOU *and* LIRA *were. He looks pleased. He gets down from the table. He goes out, left, almost running, quite delighted, saying:*

WRITER'S VOICE: I shall make an extraordinary novel out of all this. A magnificent novel! What a novel! . . .

His voice fades away in the distance. Pause. The sound of the boots of marching soldiers is heard close by. Further away, very softly, a group of men is singing 'Guernikako arbola'. The group gradually becomes more numerous and the voices gradually louder. Now a whole crowd is singing 'Guernikako arbola', which finally completely drowns the sound of the boots, as the curtain falls.

THE LABYRINTH

The great Theatre of Oklahoma calls you! Today only and never again! If you miss your chance now you miss it for ever!

Franz Kafka

CHARACTERS

ETIENNE
BRUNO
MICAELA
JUSTIN
THE JUDGE

THE LABYRINTH

A labyrinth of blankets takes up almost the whole of the stage. The blankets, like washing hung out to dry, are pegged on to wires which criss-cross over the stage in all directions.

On the right, a very small latrine, dark and dirty. It has a small window with an iron grating looking on to the space left by the blankets in the middle of the stage.

All this—all that the audience can see, that is—is only a minute part of the immense park-labyrinth formed by the blankets.

In the latrine, lying on the ground, are BRUNO *and* ETIENNE. *They are manacled together by their ankles.* BRUNO *is very ill and can hardly move. He is also very dirty and has several days' growth of beard.* ETIENNE *is dressed in a fairly clean suit; he seems in good health.* ETIENNE *is filing the manacles attaching him to* BRUNO.

BRUNO: I'm thirsty. [*Pause. It is an effort for him to speak.*] Give me some water.

ETIENNE continues his filing, trying to cut through the manacles.

[*In a very faint voice*]: I'm very thirsty.

ETIENNE is annoyed, but drags himself over to the lavatory bowl. BRUNO *utters a loud cry.* ETIENNE *pulls the chain, gets a little water in his cupped hands and gives it to* BRUNO. *He then immediately returns to the task of freeing himself. He is making great efforts; all this is obviously painful for* BRUNO, *as* ETIENNE *is pulling on the manacles with some force.* BRUNO *groans.*

ETIENNE: Don't groan so much.

He gets on with his work. BRUNO *groans again.*

31

Is that the way you help me? [*Pause.*] Make a bit of an effort, let me try and get away. [*Pause.*] It's the only way we've got left of getting some sort of justice. [*Pause.*] As soon as I've got free I'll go to the court and insist on their going into our case in detail. I won't tell them we're angels, of course, that'd be telling a lie, but I'll make them see that we've been victimised and that it's unjust.

BRUNO: I'm thirsty.

ETIENNE: Again!

BRUNO [*exhausted*]: I'm very thirsty.

ETIENNE: Wait till I've finished. When I'm free I'll give you all the water you want.

> BRUNO *groans.* ETIENNE *concentrates hard on his work, because it looks as though the manacles are about to give.* BRUNO *groans more loudly and, in spite of his weakness, starts kicking* ETIENNE *with his free leg.*

[*Extremely annoyed*]: Don't start that! Just leave me alone and stop kicking me.

BRUNO: I'm thirsty.

ETIENNE: Wait a minute.

> ETIENNE *goes on filing the manacles. Now and then he gives them a sharp tug.* BRUNO *groans more and more and kicks him.*

How can I explain? Let me get on with it. It's the only chance we've got left. Or would you rather rot in this hole for the rest of your life?

BRUNO: I'm thirsty.

ETIENNE [*annoyed*]: Oh, all right. [ETIENNE *pulls the chain and gives him some water*]. Now are you going to keep quiet? [*He goes on filing. Groan from* BRUNO.] It's almost through. [*Joyfully.*] One last effort and I'll be free.

> BRUNO *kicks him more and more, which considerably hinders* ETIENNE. *He defends himself with his head and goes on filing joyfully. Groan from* BRUNO.

BRUNO: I'm very thirsty.

ETIENNE: Just a moment.

> BRUNO *is hindering him more and more.* ETIENNE *goes*

on filing. He finally manages to file through the manacles. He's free.

BRUNO: I'm thirsty.

ETIENNE gives him some water and then immediately goes out of the latrine. In spite of his weakness, BRUNO *lifts up his hands to him to stop him.*

I'm very thirsty.

BRUNO remains stretched out in the latrine. ETIENNE, *in the park, pauses. He finally decides to penetrate into the labyrinth of blankets. So he disappears. Silence. He reappears. He goes over to the latrine window. He looks inside.* BRUNO *makes an effort and sits up with great difficulty.*

I'm thirsty.

ETIENNE is terrified, and flees. But before he penetrates into the labyrinth of blankets he pauses. He finally makes up his mind. Silence. He reappears again, quite out of breath. He looks through the bars. BRUNO *makes a great effort and sits up with difficulty.*

I'm thirsty.

ETIENNE is horrified, and flees. He goes towards the labyrinth of blankets. He hesitates, and then plunges into it. He disappears. Silence. He reappears. He goes up to the window. BRUNO *sits up.*

Hesitation. He disappears. Silence. He reappears. He repeats the operation and once again reappears, out of breath.

Silence. MICAELA *appears from the blankets.*

MICAELA: What are you doing in my park?

ETIENNE: I got lost. I'm trying to get out. [*Pause.*] I can't find the way out. I keep going round the park in between the blankets and every time I think I've found it I'm always back in the same place.

MICAELA: It's not surprising. When my father decided to hang up the washing in the park we all thought that as it was so big it would turn into a labyrinth; all the more so as they don't hang up anything but blankets.

ETIENNE: But *you'll* be able to tell me how to get out of here.

33

MICAELA: I'd be delighted to—if I only knew the way. Unfortunately, though, and in spite of all my efforts to get to know all the exits, I still haven't managed to find my way around.

ETIENNE: Why did you come as far as this then?

MICAELA: If you knew my house you wouldn't be in the least surprised. My father is a very right-minded sort of man but he was brought up very strictly, which means that everyone in the house has to be much too submissive. That's why I venture out into the park from time to time—to get away from the atmosphere in the house, even if it's only for a moment. I can tell you, to give you some idea, that everyone in the house has to dress very formally, that we are only allowed to speak in whispers, that we have to bow to him—to my father—every time we see him, that we aren't allowed to look out of the windows, that we aren't ever allowed to laugh, etc. etc. So you'll understand why I like to go for a walk in the park from time to time.

ETIENNE: But how can such a well-organised man have thought up this terrifying labyrinth of blankets?

MICAELA: You're quite right; it seems absurd, at first, but when you know the precise reasons you'll see that it isn't really so absurd. I'll tell you: this park, which is enormous, miles and miles, started off by being a playground where we could all amuse ourselves in any way we liked. The idea of turning it into a place to dry the washing occurred to my father in the most plausible way, I might almost say in the most necessary way. It was a long time since anyone had washed any of the blankets in the house—which contains, as you may know, a large number of rooms. These things start in the most ordinary way. My father had decided that each time a dirty blanket had to be changed it would be done in the simplest fashion: that is, the dirty blanket would be changed for a clean blanket and the dirty one would be put in the cellar. My father thought it would be better to wait till there were enough dirty blankets to wash them all in one go, which would be cheaper. Time went on and the blankets were gradually accumulating in the cellar. My father was horrified. He started looking for some workmen to wash the blankets but unfortunately there weren't enough in the neighbourhood at that time. So he decided to consult his friends in the capital and they immediately started looking for some workmen, while the dirty blankets, as there wasn't any more room in the cellar, started to invade the best bedrooms on the first floor. The situation was getting worse daily, there was a real danger of the blankets taking possession of the whole of the first floor, which would have been an enormous hindrance to us, because then we'd have had to have a fire escape built outside. Well, as I was saying, as the situation was daily getting worse, my father decided to go to the capital himself to engage some workmen. But unfortunately the workmen were on strike and no one was interested in my father's offer. So then he decided to promise them double pay, which didn't really satisfy them, not that the wages seemed insufficient to them but they were afraid of the anger of their comrades. In the meantime I was looking after the house and I was trying to stow the blankets in the most rational possible way, so they'd take up less room, but unfortunately, in spite of all my efforts, they went on accumulating more and more and, worst of all, there was a danger of their blocking the main staircase. I reported all this to my father in several letters, which weren't answered. I was surprised by this silence, and at his staying away so long, and telephoned him at the hotel where he was living, but they told me he'd disappeared some days before without leaving any address. This news dismayed me, all the more so as the blankets were already beginning to invade the main staircase, and the staircase that had been built to give direct access to the second floor was very unsafe and could easily collapse one fine day, which wouldn't have been so tragic if one of us had been in the road at the time, but which would have been serious if we'd all been on the second floor, because then no one would have been able to build a new staircase to

35

replace the old one. The situation, as you must see, was becoming more and more tragic. A few days later the blankets had invaded the main staircase and deprived us of half our communications, and they were seriously threatening the second floor. It was then that my father reappeared with about a hundred men, though we never found out where he'd got them from. It was odd—they were all in chains. My father explained that what with all the strikes these days it was better to force workmen to work. He immediately had some enormous boilers installed and for the next few months the workmen washed the blankets. My father thought it would be a good idea to put them in the park to dry, as it was big enough for them all to be hung up. To start with, the workmen hung them in a certain order, parallel to the boilers, but unfortunately there were so many blankets that they took up all the vacant space, so that very gradually, in a meticulous sort of way, this kind of labyrinth of blankets that the park has become came into being. And although the workmen were chained up to start with, my father took off their chains later; as the labyrinth was such a great distance between the boilers and the last clothes lines, they'd have needed exceptionally long chains, which were impossible to find. So that gradually, one by one, under cover of the night, they went away, and there wasn't a single one left. The present situation is very critical for my father: the blankets are hanging up but we can't get them taken down because of a shortage of labour. And what's more, they make a labyrinth in front of the house which almost completely stops us going out, or at least means that we have to run the risk of getting lost in it and dying of thirst, fatigue, and exhaustion. And then, for the moment, we can't count on recruiting the necessary workmen (a hundred, two hundred, maybe a thousand or more, my father is the only one who knows) to take down the blankets and pile them up properly so they don't start getting in our way again. As you can see, there's nothing at all pleasant about this situation, especially for us who have to suffer the direct consequences of it. But you're only passing through here and you can't realise what it's all like.

A pause. She stares ostentatiously at the manacle round his ankle.

Unless you're here for good.

ETIENNE [*awkwardly hiding the manacle with his other leg*]: Of course I'm not, I'm not here for good.

MICAELA: I hope that's how it is. It would be very surprising if you were to be at the house or in the park for good without my knowing you. Because my father knows everyone who lives in the house very well, but I think I can say without fear of being mistaken that I know them all, too—or nearly all.

BRUNO [*who is still lying on the latrine floor, says plaintively*]: I'm very thirsty. [*Pause.*] Give me some water, Etienne.

ETIENNE *is obviously nervous, and tries to pretend.* MICAELA *has heard* BRUNO'S *voice. She looks perfectly natural and doesn't seem at all surprised.*

MICAELA: We have to take my father's perfect organisation into account. We can be quite sure that nothing happens in the house or in this park that he doesn't know about. There only needs to be one blanket missing, only one— and just think, there must be millions and millions in the park—for him to notice at once, and if he doesn't immediately, in person, take the matter up with whoever has stolen it, it's simply because at that moment his time is very precious, he's busy with other, much more important things. But there isn't the slightest doubt that sooner or later, according to an order which is too complicated for me, and incomprehensible, he will deal with the matter and settle it with perfect impartiality, taking into consideration, one by one, all the circumstances which either incriminate or vindicate the accused. That's why ...

BRUNO [*interrupting her*]: I'm very thirsty.

Silence. ETIENNE *is nervous.* MICAELA *is completely calm.*

37

MICAELA: As I was saying, that's why things here may appear to be in some disorder, but it is an apparent disorder which only throws into relief the existence of a superior order which is much more complex and exigent than any we can imagine. My father controls it with a skill which is of exceptional efficiency.

ETIENNE: Then how do you explain this labyrinth of blankets, which came into being, according to what you say, because your father showed such a lack of foresight that he let the blankets pile up in the cellar, and even obstruct the entrance to the house?

BRUNO: I'm thirsty.

Same business.

MICAELA: I consider that a fair question, and I would have asked myself the same thing a thousand times if I didn't know my father, but the solution is much simpler than that. I've already told you that my father observes a strict order in the affairs he deals with, which sometimes leads him to solve some problems which seem insignificant to us but which must be seen to before others, which we imagine to be more important. This is merely a consequence of the difference between our scale of values and that of my father. For instance, I told you that when the pile of blankets had risen so dangerously up to the first floor, I telephoned his hotel, where they told me that he was away. Gone without leaving an address. After making detailed enquiries, I heard, though perhaps it wasn't correct, that my father had spent a month in a town a long way away, forgetting the business of the blankets, and completely absorbed in picking certain herbs reputed to cure chilblains. I mean it when I say that I'm not sure of the accuracy of the facts, because my father's life is a real mystery, but there's a good chance of them being true. In any case, this way of behaving is peculiarly his own, and I could give you a thousand other examples of the same sort. The case I've told you of is a perfect illustration of what I was trying to prove to you, which is that my father has a scale of values which is different from

38

ours and that his priorities obey a rigorous and impenetrable system which, in spite of its absurdity, turns out to be the best in the long run, as I've been able to observe a thousand times.

BRUNO: I'm very thirsty.

Silence. MICAELA *gets up and goes over to the latrine.*

ETIENNE: Where are you going?

MICAELA: There.

She points to the latrine.

ETIENNE: I don't think that's necessary. Is something worrying you? Tell me what's surprising you and I'll explain everything.

MICAELA: I don't see why anything should be surprising me. Why d'you think I should be surprised?

ETIENNE: No reason, no reason.

ETIENNE *tries awkwardly to stop* MICAELA *going over to the latrine; he even goes so far as to grab her by the arm.* MICAELA *manages to free herself and goes into the latrine.* ETIENNE *anxiously watches her through the latrine window.* MICAELA *pulls the chain. She watches the water flow with profound satisfaction.* BRUNO *sits up a bit with a painful effort, and in spite of his suffering and his thirst, says nothing.* MICAELA *goes out of the latrine. She avoids walking on* BRUNO, *who is by the entrance. She goes back to* ETIENNE.

MICAELA [*continuing the conversation*]: As I was saying, my father's order is a complete enigma for us. How could anyone justify spending his time picking herbs for chilblains when the situation in the house was becoming tragic because of the blankets, especially if you take into account the fact that no one in the house ever has chilblains and that, on the other hand, the efficacy of these herbs has been denied in the most categorical fashion by the best doctors, who even go so far as to state that the value of these herbs is based on superstition and witchcraft.

ETIENNE: Yes. [*Worried.*] But how shall I be able to get out of here?

39

MICAELA: Unless you're very lucky, or get direct help from my father, you needn't hope to get out.

ETIENNE: I could get out of here with you.

MICAELA [*with a compassionate smile*]: Impossible; unfortunately, it's impossible.

ETIENNE: Can't you get out either, then?

MICAELA: Of course I can. Would I venture into the labyrinth if I couldn't get out again?

ETIENNE: Well then—when you leave here, let me come with you.

MICAELA: That's something I couldn't do for you, even if it was what I wanted most in all the world. My father, who, as I've told you, has organised everything to perfection, has managed to work out a very cunning scheme to enable me to get back to the house even if I happen to be in the remotest part of the labyrinth. This scheme, like all my father's schemes, by the way, is simple but effective. It's this bell [*she produces a little bell*]—every time I want to go back I ring it until one of the servants who knows the labyrinth appears. A servant who is dumb, and so can't reveal its secret to anyone.

ETIENNE: How many servants are there?

MICAELA: That's something I've never been able to find out. So far it's always been a different servant who's come and fetched me, which means that there must be more than a thousand, maybe even more, but maybe less—my calculations in these matters are only guesswork, which means that I may well be wrong; in any case they're all dumb, and none of them has ever been able to tell me the secret of the way back to the house, a secret my father must have revealed to them.

ETIENNE: But none of this stops me coming with you.

MICAELA: Let me finish my explanation. Your questions, as always, are reasonable. That's why I have to explain to you in detail—well, with all the precision I'm capable of —every little factor of every problem, to arrive at an accurate and comprehensible solution. As I told you,

40

when I ring the bell a servant arrives in a surprisingly short time, sometimes ten minutes, sometimes just a few seconds, while I'll have been walking in the labyrinth for hours and hours, and he leads me to the house. It's all the same to me whether you come with me or not, but there are insuperable obstacles. In the first place you have to take into account the extreme susceptibility of the servant, who is prepared to serve the people who belong to the house but not strangers, which is logical. How do you suppose I could make him serve you—*you*, an outsider? I could, of course, *try* to ask him, just to do you a favour, even though I know beforehand that the chances of his accepting such a responsibility are extremely remote. But that's not the worst. As the labyrinth is tortuous, and the blankets are almost touching each other, they're so close together—you must have noticed that you can only make any progress by moving them one at a time—it's absolutely impossible for the servant to guide two people. Every time I've tried it the person with me has disappeared very shortly after starting to walk between the blankets and, later on, the servants have found his dead body. As you'll realise, it means taking a completely useless risk: if you come with me you won't have the slightest chance of getting out of the labyrinth but, on the other hand, there'll be every likelihood of your dying of thirst and fatigue. If you try to get out on your own, the difficulties are the same but the risks less, because as people have a natural sense of direction they manage to come back to their point of departure, that's to say to this sort of island, without running the risk of dying of hunger in the labyrinth. But if you follow the servant you'll make so much headway in a few seconds—I've already told you that he can travel a surprising distance in a few seconds, because of my father's system, I suppose—that when you've got lost you won't be able to find this refuge again. It's the only privileged place in the labyrinth, and it's exactly in the centre of the park, as you may perhaps know.

41

BRUNO: I'm thirsty.

    Silence.

MICAELA: As you'll have been able to realise, this business of the blankets has caused us nothing but trouble from the very beginning, and, unfortunately, there's extremely little likelihood of the situation getting any better.

BRUNO: I'm thirsty.

    MICAELA *goes into the latrine, trying to avoid* BRUNO. *Pulls the chain. She watches the water flow with profound satisfaction.* ETIENNE *watches her through the window.* BRUNO *makes a supreme effort and raises himself very slightly. He says nothing.* MICAELA *goes out of the latrine. She goes back to* ETIENNE.

MICAELA: We really haven't had much luck; things have gradually got more and more complicated in a simple, but implacable fashion.

    She stares ostentatiously at the manacle round ETIENNE'S *ankle.* ETIENNE *hides it awkwardly by putting his other leg on top of it.*

You've managed to break the chain, at least.

ETIENNE: What chain?

MICAELA: What chain do you think? The one you were tied up by over there.

ETIENNE [*after a pause, anxiously*]: Yes.

MICAELA: It's always the same. I'm sick and tired of telling him that that method's no good, that it's easy to file through manacles, but he never listens to me. Well, after all, it's all the same to me. Whether manacles can be filed through or not, whether it's a good method or not, doesn't matter much. [*Pause.*] And, naturally, you want to get out of here as soon as possible.

ETIENNE: Yes.

MICAELA: That's logical. [*Pause.*] But it seems to me to be very difficult. As I've already explained.

ETIENNE: It's not impossible, then?

MICAELA: Impossible, really impossible . . . everything in life is possible.

42

BRUNO: I'm very thirsty.

> MICAELA, *slightly annoyed, as if she's had enough, gets up. She goes to the latrine. She avoids* BRUNO *as she goes in. She pulls the chain. She watches the water flow with profound satisfaction.* ETIENNE *watches her through the window.* BRUNO *tries to sit up. He says nothing.* MICAELA *goes out of the latrine. She comes back to* ETIENNE.

MICAELA: As I say, it's quite obvious that nothing in life is impossible, but what you want to do is one of the most difficult things to put into practice. To prove my good faith, and the sincerity of my offers, I'm going to do everything it's in my power to do for you: call my father, so that he can find the best solution for you himself.

> MICAELA *produces a little bell and makes a very faint sound with it twice.*

ETIENNE: Do you think they'll have heard the bell at the house?

MICAELA: Of course not. Even if the bell rang much more loudly they wouldn't hear it from the house. The distance between us and them is immense! But to remedy this drawback my father has invented a rather ingenious system: he's posted a series of servants all along the park —I've never seen them, you must realise—who pass on, from one to the other, until it gets to the house, the call, or it might be the information, that my father wants to hear. All this is done with fantastic speed, so that my father knows what is going on at the remotest parts of the labyrinth without the slightest delay. The whole thing, now, is to find out whether he wants to come immediately or whether we'll have to wait long for him. If you climb up on to my shoulders you'll be able to find out; you'll see over the blankets whether he's coming or not. Unfortunately the blankets get higher and higher, so you won't be able to see anything beyond a radius of a hundred yards. Come on, then.

ETIENNE: You want me to climb on to your shoulders?

MICAELA: Yes, you'll see whether my father's coming.

ETIENNE: I'm heavy.

43

MICAELA: Doesn't matter, I'm used to it. The last time there
was a flood my father made me carry all the servants to
safety on my shoulders. At first this work seemed ex-
hausting; I had to carry each servant nearly two miles,
leave him in the shelter and then rush back to the house
to get the next one. But I got used to it in the end, and at
the end of a month I can say that I didn't feel the weight
any more.

> MICAELA *grabs* ETIENNE *roughly by the arm and pulls
> him over to the latrine.*

Climb on my shoulders.

> ETIENNE *climbs on to* MICAELA'S *shoulders and leans
> against the wall.*

Can you see anything?

ETIENNE: No.

MICAELA: Look again.

ETIENNE [*anxiously*]: But . . . who is it?

MICAELA: It must be my father, it can't be anyone else.

ETIENNE [*full of anxiety*]: But that's the man who put me
in the lavatory and put the manacles on me.

> ETIENNE *tries to escape.* MICAELA *brutally grabs his legs,
> paralysing them with her arms.*

[*In anguish*]: Let me escape. Do let me.

MICAELA [*calmly, but without releasing* ETIENNE'S *legs*]: You
see my father's meticulous organisation. I called him a
few minutes ago and here he is already. One really can
say that there is not the slightest doubt that he controls
absolutely everything that goes on in the park.

> *Enter the Father.* ETIENNE *gets down from* MICAELA'S
> *shoulders.* JUSTIN, *the father, kisses his daughter*
> MICAELA *ceremoniously on the forehead.* ETIENNE
> *is absolutely terrified and doesn't know what to do or
> say. He hesitates. Then, as* JUSTIN *and* MICAELA *seem to
> be looking the other way for a moment, he tries to
> escape.* MICAELA *brutally holds him back by the arm.*
> JUSTIN *who, up till then, had appeared not to have
> noticed* ETIENNE'S *presence, goes over to him calmly and
> courteously.*

JUSTIN: What do you want, young man?

MICAELA: He must have been shut up in the lavatory, look at the manacle still hanging from his ankle—[ETIENNE *tries awkwardly to hide it*] he's managed to break it. Now he wants at all costs to escape from the park, and he's tried to buy me in every possible way to achieve his end. First of all he promised me a vast sum of money if I'd help him get out of the park.

> ETIENNE *tries to protest.* JUSTIN *takes not the slightest notice of what he does. Nor does* MICAELA.

Then he proposed marriage to me, he tried to seduce me in the most lamentable fashion, and finally he submitted to me a plan of rebellion against your authority in which the two of us would seize the house and park.

ETIENNE [*excitedly*]: Monsieur, please don't believe . . .

> *No one is listening to him.*

JUSTIN: And what was the young man's plan?

MICAELA: You can imagine it: a piece of rank stupidity, devoid of the most elementary common sense. He wanted me to help him set fire to the park, because he maintained that as blankets burn very easily the fire would soon assume gigantic proportions and the park and house would be completely destroyed. And when everything was razed to the ground and the servants, and everyone else in the house, dead—and you too, of course —we could sell most of the park and, with the money we'd get for it, build a new house where he and I and a few servants would live.

JUSTIN: Yes, it really is lamentable.

ETIENNE: But, Monsieur . . .

MICAELA: Naturally I didn't listen to any of his suggestions, and I was all the time trying to dissuade him from them.

JUSTIN: You did well; individuals of this sort are very dangerous, especially when one allows oneself to be deceived by their appearance of being so calm and good, which conceals their perfidious intentions. Leave him to me, my girl, his punishment will fit his crime. I shall deal with this matter personally. [*Pause.*] Now, if you like, you may go and see your fiancé.

JUSTIN *kisses her ceremoniously on the forehead.* MICAELA *goes into the latrine where* BRUNO *is. She sits down by him and caresses him passionately.* BRUNO *takes absolutely no notice of her.* JUSTIN *and* ETIENNE *remain in the middle of the stage.*

I must ask you, young man, to excuse my daughter. Take it in good part. [*He sighs.*] There's nothing that can be done about it, all I ask is that you don't contradict her, so as not to aggravate her mental imbalance. In any case, as a rule everything she says is of very little importance; her evidence has almost no chance of being accepted by any court.

ETIENNE: If that's the case, Monsieur, I completely absolve her, but I can assure you that while she was inventing all those tales against me I couldn't stop myself hating her with all my heart.

JUSTIN: I'm very grateful to you for being so understanding about her.

ETIENNE: Was it all lies too then, what she told me about the labyrinth?

JUSTIN: It was and it wasn't. She made some colossal mistakes which could have misled you, not out of malice or because she needs to tell lies, but because she doesn't remember things very well. Her memory is very poor and she forgets all the most important details, or else changes them, and substitutes other very precise facts for them. For instance, she told you that I spent a month in a town a long way away, while the blankets were piling up and becoming dangerous, picking herbs to cure chilblains. That's completely untrue: actually I spent a month in that town picking herbs to cure corns, and not chilblains, as she twice asserted. That's why we must excuse her, we must take a generous view of what she says, and never get angry. That's what I do, and what I'm asking you to do too.

ETIENNE [*very humbly*]: Yes, I promise you I won't get cross.

JUSTIN: Well, now we've cleared up the first important point, let's move on to the next. You want to get out of the park, don't you?

ETIENNE: Yes, Monsieur.

JUSTIN: My daughter has already explained to you the rather unusual circumstances we are in because of the blankets. You can't imagine how much I regret that you should be a victim, even temporarily, of this situation. Believe me, I deplore it even more than you do. Do you realise the delicate situation I am in in relation to my guests, my prisoners, my servants, and the friends who come to the house? There's not the slightest doubt that that's one of my gravest worries at the moment.

ETIENNE: I can understand you.

JUSTIN: I don't know if you are aware of it, but every day thousands and thousands of people pass through my house, guests, prisoners . . . [*a pause.* ETIENNE *looks absolutely terrified.* JUSTIN *goes on calmly*] . . . friends, clients.

Silence.

MICAELA [*to* BRUNO]: Kiss me, my love.

MICAELA is sprawling in an obscene fashion by BRUNO'S side in the latrine. He is still lying down, and takes no notice. She caresses him.

[*To* BRUNO]: Caress me, caress my breasts, Bruno. My body belongs to you.

In the park, JUSTIN *watches his daughter through the window with a certain satisfaction.* ETIENNE *is near* JUSTIN, *and also watches what is going on. In the latrine,* MICAELA *is still obscenely sprawling all over* BRUNO, *who still takes no notice.* MICAELA *tries to excite* BRUNO *by obscene imprecations. She kisses him on his mouth and on his belly.*

JUSTIN: [*very satisfied, to* ETIENNE]: You can't imagine how delighted I am at my daughter's romantic behaviour. [*He is still watching the scene. Groans from* MICAELA. *Kisses. Caresses.*] She's a child, she doesn't see any harm in it, she's just a child. I'm completely satisfied. I'm lucky to have a daughter like that. Especially these days, when everything's so unstable. [*With great enthusiasm.*] A child. Just a child! Innocence personified. [MICAELA *obscene,* BRUNO *impassive, etc.*] It's such a touching love story. All the more so if you take into account the highly unusual circumstances that have, and still do, beset them. But let's not change the subject. It's a real problem getting out of the park, as you know very well, but there is, fortunately, a solution to it. It's very complicated, it's true, but still it's a solution. In principle your case has to be dealt with by a judge who represents the Supreme Tribunal, given that you have that manacle on your ankle, which doesn't make matters any easier for you, as I might as well tell you from the start.

ETIENNE: But I'm wearing this manacle, not because I've done anything wrong, or committed any crime, but just because . . . [*he hesitates*] . . . just as an ornament.

JUSTIN: You needn't worry in the slightest. In actual fact you'll appear before the Supreme Tribunal—I mean, of course, before the judge representing it—simply to comply with a bureaucratic formality. If, as you state, you aren't guilty, the judge, after a superficial investigation and after he's filled in the requisite forms, will immediately set you free, and allow you the help of the servants, who will do their best to lead you out of the labyrinth.

ETIENNE: I'd like to get out as soon as possible, because I'm in a hurry. Can't I avoid the court formalities?

Obscene gestures from MICAELA *in the latrine.*

MICAELA: Kiss me, I'm yours.

MICAELA *is obscene,* BRUNO *is impassive, and at death's door.* JUSTIN *looks pleased.*

JUSTIN: That's impossible—absolutely impossible. The judge has to carry out his investigation not only on account of that accursed manacle, which makes you suspect from the start, but also to comply with the regulations.

ETIENNE: I don't see the point.

JUSTIN: The judge has to give you an exit permit, after the

usual investigation; this has been the rule ever since they discovered how little the law was respected. Because, after considerable research, they managed to discover that, in a single year, eleven thousand people against whom proceedings were pending had got out of the park, and most of them were accused of very serious offences, what's more. This was because there had been no check on people coming into or going out of the park. I remember distinctly that in those days you only had to ask for an exit permit to get one immediately. Fortunately they've put a stop to all that: now everyone coming into and going out of the park has to be investigated by the judge.

ETIENNE: And do I have to be investigated by the judge too?

JUSTIN: Naturally. There are no exceptions. I've already told you that there was a great deal of abuse, that's why the judges are so severe now. Perhaps a bit too much so, but however you look at it, it's necessary. What I can do for you is speed up the proceedings.

ETIENNE: How d'you mean, speed up the proceedings?

JUSTIN: I mean that I can try and arrange for your hearing to take place as soon as possible. In general you have to wait at least a month.

ETIENNE: I can't wait that long.

JUSTIN: They nearly always say: I can't wait that long. But what do you suppose they can do, when the number of trials is increasing all the time? Do you imagine they can settle them all just like that?

ETIENNE: It's not my fault if there are more trials.

JUSTIN: No, in theory, it's not your fault. And yet, if we were to examine the problem a little more closely, we should come to the conclusion in the end that, like all the other individuals who have passed through the park, you *are* guilty—indirectly, if you like, of this state of affairs. You are neither more nor less than one more link in the chain that has been formed, is being formed, and will continue to be formed, out of the increasing number of cases investigated by the tribunal. I told you I'd try and have your case dealt with as soon as possible.

There's a trick I'll play. [*Pause.* JUSTIN's *expression is ironic.*] A trick which, naturally enough, is perfectly legal, because you will quite understand that I wouldn't break the law, even to help you. I'll explain. The judges have had very strict orders that they are always to deal with these matters in strict chronological order. Exceptions can be made, though, if I remember rightly, in the following case: if the individuals found in the park are thought liable to be subject to another tribunal, then they may appear immediately. And this, precisely, applies in your case: the manacle round your ankle makes you particularly suspect. Thanks to this detail you'll be able, legally, to be dealt with by the tribunal before your turn.

ETIENNE: Good. That's what I want.

JUSTIN: I must warn you that this provision is a two-edged weapon, because the judges of the emergency tribunal who investigate cases like yours are very severe. They have some excuse: they're used to trying criminals of the worst type, who maintain their innocence with the greatest cynicism. That's why they tend to be suspicious at first, I might even go so far as to say that they take no notice of the testimony of the accused. But after all, it isn't too serious if they make a mistake because the accused goes on afterwards to the higher tribunal, and they do consider the evidence when they try him.

ETIENNE: I've nothing to be afraid of.

JUSTIN: Quite: we shouldn't exaggerate. And anyway, this first tribunal, as I told you, is only concerned with fact-finding, and it's very rare for it to condemn the accused directly.

ETIENNE: But this tribunal *can* condemn people?

JUSTIN: I've already told you that in theory it only enquires into the facts of the case, but in certain cases, where there is absolutely no doubt of the accused's guilt, or when he is obviously dangerous, the tribunal takes it upon itself to decide to punish him without reference to the higher tribunal. The punishment can sometimes, even, be the death penalty.

Silence. MICAELA, *in the latrine, is still obscenely wrapping herself round* BRUNO.

ETIENNE: Doesn't matter, I want to get out as quickly as possible.

JUSTIN: You can choose: either you wait your turn, or else you can be tried quickly by the emergency tribunal which will treat you, as I told you, very severely, all the more so as it will take your manacle into account. Tell me which you prefer.

ETIENNE: To be tried as soon as possible.

MICAELA [*still obscenely kissing* BRUNO *in the latrine*]: Kiss me, kiss my thighs.

JUSTIN *looks pleased.*

JUSTIN [*pointing to the latrine*]: Isn't that sweet? [*A pause.*] Excuse me, I get so easily sidetracked. We were saying ... ah yes, you say you want to be tried by the emergency tribunal.

ETIENNE: Yes, Monsieur.

JUSTIN: Would you like me to go now and fetch the judge who investigates cases like yours?

ETIENNE: Yes, if you can.

JUSTIN: I'll go at once, then. I can't promise to come back immediately because the judge may not be in his office for the moment and I may have to wait for him. Anyway, I'll do my best to come back with him as soon as possible. [*Pause.*] You see how these things are—I too am curious about your case and I shall be interested to hear the verdict. So ...

JUSTIN *looks delighted. He goes over to the latrine window, through which he watches* MICAELA, *still tangled up with* BRUNO.

Goodbye then, young man.

ETIENNE: Goodbye, Monsieur.

JUSTIN *gets lost among the blankets.* MICAELA *stops embracing* BRUNO *and smoothes down her clothes. She comes out of the latrine quickly and goes over to the blankets. She listens carefully. Silence.*

MICAELA: He's gone. [*She seems excited.*]

51

ETIENNE: But he said he'd be back very soon.

MICAELA: You never know.

ETIENNE: How d'you mean, you never know?

MICAELA: Yes, you never know for certain whether he'll be back at once or a long time after.

ETIENNE [*incredulous*]: Yes, of course.

MICAELA: Don't you believe me?

ETIENNE: Of course I believe you.

MICAELA: I'm not joking, I've known lots of cases like yours and I'm only too well aware of it.

ETIENNE: Naturally.

MICAELA: I can see you don't believe me.

ETIENNE: But I do—I do believe you.

MICAELA: No, don't pretend, I know what's going on. My father told you I was mad and that you must humour me. Didn't he? [*Silence.*] And anyway, you must resent my inventing all those bad things about you. Don't you? [*Silence.*] Tell me the truth.

ETIENNE: Naturally: do you suppose I liked it?

MICAELA: You mustn't attach so much importance to it.

ETIENNE: I don't attach the slightest importance to it.

MICAELA: You're quite right. It's not my fault. My father forces me to say all those things.

ETIENNE [*suspicious*]: Of course.

MICAELA: Don't say it like that. I'm telling you the truth. My father forces me to.

Silence. MICAELA *weeps.*

ETIENNE [*touched*]: Don't cry. [*Pause.*] What can I do for you? I tell you, I believe you.

MICAELA [*sighing*]: You're only trying to cheer me up.

Silence. ETIENNE *hesitates.*

My father forces me to tell all those unlikely tales so that afterwards he can show how generous he is, and that's how he gets everything he wants. People start by being suspicious of what I say, and then he passes for someone who loves his daughter dearly.

Silence. MICAELA *weeps. She bares her back. It is covered with blood and bears obvious marks of the whip.*

Look.

ETIENNE, *horrified, examines* MICAELA'S *back.*

MICAELA: Touch it, touch it.

MICAELA *makes* ETIENNE *touch her back. He gets blood on his hand.*

You see the blood.

ETIENNE [*impressed*]: Yes.

MICAELA: My father did that to me.

ETIENNE: He can't have.

MICAELA: He whips me every day. [*Sobbing.*] And he says he'll beat me more if I don't do everything he wants. That's why when he's there I have to say everything he's told me to say beforehand. This morning he made me pretend to be mad in front of you, I couldn't do anything but obey him. Otherwise he'd have beaten me worse than usual tonight.

ETIENNE [*deeply moved*]: It's intolerable.

MICAELA: Yes, but what can I do?

ETIENNE: Run away.

MICAELA: That's impossible.

ETIENNE: What d'you mean, impossible?

MICAELA: My father would stop me. And in any case I wouldn't know where to go. I'd starve to death. At least my father feeds me. [*She weeps.* ETIENNE *is moved.*] And in any case, he isn't my father. He makes me call him my father and he calls me his daughter when other people are there, but he isn't really my father. Everything he does is so as to get a good reputation.

ETIENNE [*resolutely*]: I'll get you out of here.

MICAELA [*sadly*]: It'll be very difficult. And anyway, you'll have enough trouble saving yourself.

ETIENNE: Why?

MICAELA: I heard my father telling you you'd be tried by the emergency tribunal judge. He's a very cruel judge who finds practically everyone who comes up before him guilty. During the hearing of the case he treats the accused with contempt and he's quite merciless. He hardly even allows them to speak or defend themselves;

he pees on them, sticks pins into them, belches into their mouths, ties them hand and foot, and even bites them, sometimes. It's true too, though, that in other circumstances he can be extremely polite to them, but this is rare. The worst thing is that no one, or practically no one, ever gets off.

ETIENNE: Ah, but *I* shall—I'm innocent. I haven't done anything wrong. [*Pause.*] When I'm free I shall get you out of here.

MICAELA [*touched*]: Thank you very much. You're very good to me.

ETIENNE: I can't allow your father to treat you like that.

> BRUNO, *in the latrine, gets up. He goes over to the lavatory chain.*

MICAELA: You mustn't worry about me, you must try and escape without bothering about me. You can see very well all the difficulties involved, you'll have your work cut out just trying to get away from here on your own.

> BRUNO, *in the latrine, has reached the chain. He hangs himself from it. The weight of his body makes the water in the tank overflow.* ETIENNE *and* MICAELA *are much affected, and say nothing for a moment.*

MICAELA: Did you hear that?

ETIENNE: Yes. [*He goes over to the latrine and looks at* BRUNO'*s corpse in horror.*]

MICAELA: He's hanged himself. [*Silence.*] It was only to be expected. [*Silence.* MICAELA *suddenly goes over to the corpse.*] Help me.

> MICAELA *and* ETIENNE *between them take down the body. They carry the body to the centre of the stage. Silence. They contemplate the body. Silence.* MICAELA, *in meditative mood, respectfully takes one of* BRUNO'S *hands. She kisses it. She may be crying. Silence.* MICAELA *covers* BRUNO'S *face with a handkerchief.*

We must hide the body.

ETIENNE: Hide it. Why?

MICAELA: If the judge sees a corpse here he'll accuse you of murder. Help me.

ETIENNE: What d'you want me to do?

MICAELA: We'll put the corpse in the furthest possible place from here.

ETIENNE: Right, I'll help you.

MICAELA: That's the best way to make a body disappear. The park's so big that it'll be almost impossible for anyone to find it. Help me, take his legs.

ETIENNE: Let me take his shoulders, they're heavier.

MICAELA: No, do what I say.

They lift BRUNO *up, take him off and disappear among the blankets. Silence. No one on the stage.* ETIENNE *and* MICAELA *reappear.*

MICAELA: I don't think anyone will find him.

ETIENNE: And if someone does find him, what'll happen?

MICAELA: Your cause will be lost.

Silence.

ETIENNE: When did Bruno arrive in the lavatory?

MICAELA: I don't know. Every time I've been here I've found him tied up. Since I was a very small child.

ETIENNE: And weren't you sorry for him?

MICAELA: Yes, I was at first, I used to come here every morning and pee in front of him because he liked that. He looked quite happy when he watched me. Then we'd play together, I'd bring some buckets of sand and he'd bury my feet. [*Pause.*] But it was very difficult to play with him because he was always tied up and very ill.

ETIENNE: Has he always been ill?

MICAELA: Yes, always. He used to bleed all the time and no one ever changed his clothes. The blood used to dry on his shirt and suit. [*Pause.*] I used to bring him chocolate, and almonds, too, to give him a treat, and needles, lots of needles, especially.

ETIENNE: What did he want needles for?

MICAELA: To prick me with. When I was small he used to prick my legs, and when I became a woman he'd only prick my breasts and my stomach

ETIENNE: And you let him do it?

MICAELA: Of course, why not?

55

ETIENNE: But it must have been very painful.

MICAELA: Yes, very. It was almost unbearable. [*Pause.*] And then he wouldn't let me cry, or scream.

ETIENNE: But why did you go and see him?

MICAELA: I was terribly bored. When I was with him I got hurt, but at least I wasn't bored.

ETIENNE: He was a monster, then.

MICAELA: That wasn't the worst. The worst thing was that he used to tell my father all about it afterwards. [*Pause.*] My father had strictly forbidden me to go and see him, and particularly to take him anything. Well, he always used to tell, and my father would beat me.

ETIENNE: Your father told me you were his fiancée.

MICAELA: That's just a figure of speech. I wasn't really, but my father liked to tell everyone I was his fiancée, because, on the other hand, it wasn't completely false either. That's why he ordered me to kiss him and take him in my arms as passionately as possible when strangers were there. It was never passionate enough for his liking.

ETIENNE: And were you going to marry him?

MICAELA: No, not that. It wouldn't have been possible to marry him. He couldn't ever have left the lavatory.

ETIENNE: Why not?

MICAELA: Only my father knows that. My father told me that he came into the park one day like you did, and that he'd been here ever since.

ETIENNE: Was he found guilty by the judge?

MICAELA: I don't know. We never know much about that sort of thing.

ETIENNE: He told me that he was innocent and that I must intercede for him.

MICAELA: Yes, he used to say the same to everyone.

ETIENNE: How d'you mean, to everyone?

MICAELA: Yes, to everyone who spent a few days with him in the lavatory.

ETIENNE: He told me he'd always been on his own.

MICAELA: Yes, he had. That didn't stop him now and then

56

having a companion chained to him by the ankle, though. But all his companions always managed to file through the chain and escape, so he always got left on his own.

ETIENNE: And what happened to them?

MICAELA: My father will have dealt with them. I don't think any of them ever managed to get out.

Silence. ETIENNE *looks tragic.* MICAELA *pulls an enormous comb out of her pocket and combs her hair coquettishly.*

They were all extremely nice. [*Pause.*] They were sorry for me and promised to get me out of here. [*Pause.*] Always full of hope. It was a pleasure to come and have a chat with them.

Enter JUSTIN. *He doesn't speak. He waits, impassively.* MICAELA *has her back turned to her father; she makes fun of him and puts out her tongue at him.* ETIENNE *is scared and signals to* MICAELA *to stop making fun of him.* JUSTIN *intercepts his signals to* MICAELA *and stares at him reproachfully. Noises off: it seems that someone is moving some heavy furniture. The* JUDGE *appears; he comes in backwards, dragging after him a small table with a large drawer in it. Attached to the table, like railway carriages to an engine, are four chairs. The* JUDGE *has a bottle in one pocket; he is very dirty. He has a fairly long beard.* ETIENNE *studies him with animosity.* MICAELA *doesn't look at the* JUDGE, *but goes on putting out her tongue at her father. The* JUDGE, *fussily, but awkwardly, detaches the chairs. He sets out the table and chairs, in what are presumably their predetermined places (he does it with a great deal of care, guessing at the correct distances separating them, etc.).*

JUDGE: Take your seats.

ETIENNE *is about to sit down on one of the chairs.*

[*Violently*]:No, not yet.

ETIENNE *stands up again apprehensively. The* JUDGE *takes the chair* ETIENNE *was going to sit on, looks at him angrily—and puts it behind the table. He sits down on it. The table and chairs are distributed thus:*

☐	Judge's chair
☐	Table

Justin's chair ☐
Micaela's chair ☐   ☐ Etienne's chair

JUDGE: Take your seats.

> *No one sits down.*

Didn't you hear what I said?

> ETIENNE, *trembling, sits down on one of the chairs to the left. The* JUDGE, *furiously angry, gets up, grabs him violently by the jacket and moves him over to the chair on the right.* MICAELA *and* JUSTIN *then immediately sit down on the chairs on the left:* MICAELA *on the one furthest away from the* JUDGE *and* JUSTIN, *therefore, on the other. The* JUDGE *sits down on the chair behind the table. The* JUDGE *takes all sorts of papers out of his pockets and puts them methodically on the table: when he puts one in the wrong place he corrects his mistake. Then he brings a bottle of wine out of another pocket and puts it on the ground by his chair. Finally he brings out a big sausage sandwich wrapped in newspaper. During the whole of the hearing he eats his sandwich very slowly and monotonously. He nibbles at it, rather than eats it.*

JUDGE [*suddenly addresses* ETIENNE, *pointing his finger at him*]: I have been vaguely informed about your case. I hope you aren't going to make me waste too much time and that you'll state the facts as concisely as possible and with all the necessary exactitude.

> ETIENNE *is about to speak.*

[*Interrupting him*]: If I tell you to state your case as concisely as possible it is because I wish sentence to be passed without delay. But if you need to call witnesses to support your evidence, have no fear; even if they are a long way away we shall have them brought here. The motto of the emergency tribunal is: severity and justice.

ETIENNE *is comforted.*

Begin.

ETIENNE: In actual fact, your worship, I don't think there's any case for you to hear.

The JUDGE *is surprised and irritated, and sits up with a gesture of disapproval.* MICAELA *is very pleased and makes approving gestures.*

I simply got lost in the park, and I want to get out of it as soon as I can. I'm within my rights, I think. The master of the house has no option but to let me go. It's truly inconceivable—that anyone who owns this property should make difficulties when people get lost in one of his parks and want to get out.

JUSTIN *is hanging his head, and seems impressed.* MICAELA *encourages* ETIENNE. *She sends him kisses with her hand. The* JUDGE *nibbles at his sandwich.*

JUDGE: In principle, I have nothing against your request . . . [*he picks up his bottle and uncorks it*] . . . Which I should say is quite justified. [*He drinks a little wine out of the bottle.*] But there's one extremely serious detail; I am speaking, as you have probably guessed, of your manacle.

ETIENNE: The manacle . . . that's just for appearances. I wear it on my ankle like a piece of jewellery. What's surprising about that?

MICAELA *is full of enthusiasm and encourages* ETIENNE.

JUDGE: No, really, there's nothing surprising about that.

Pause. He nibbles. He shakes off the crumbs. His beard is full of them.

We've seen odder things than that. [*Pause.*] At my age, as you can imagine, I've seen just about everything.

Pause. He nibbles. He points at ETIENNE *and speaks in an accusing tone of voice.*

You didn't get lost in the park, you were put in the lavatory by the owner of the house [*pointing to* JUSTIN] who chained you up there with that manacle.

He calms down. He drinks a mouthful of wine. He nibbles. MICAELA *is sad,* JUSTIN *is pleased. Silence.*

59

ETIENNE: Yes, it's true. He chained me up.

JUDGE [*going through the same routine*]: Were you alone in the latrine?

ETIENNE: Yes.

JUDGE [*bored*]: You mean to say that no one was chained up with you?

ETIENNE: Yes. I was by myself. That was why I wanted to escape. I was terribly bored. He had no reason to chain me up, that was why I wanted to escape. [*Pause.*] I filed through the chain and I managed to escape;

JUDGE [*to himself*]: Those manacles are no good.

ETIENNE: It was very difficult.

JUDGE: Nothing was more natural than to try and escape. I'd have done the same, in your situation. Being chained up all by yourself in that latrine can't be very amusing. If you'd had a companion it would have been another matter. People can always find something to say to each other, can't they? [*Silence.*] I'm asking you whether you don't agree with me?

ETIENNE [*in a strangled voice*]: Yes.

> The JUDGE *nibbles. He gets up from his chair and goes over to* ETIENNE. *He says to him, politely.*

JUDGE: Excuse me. Get up a moment.

> The JUDGE *changes his position so that he is now directly facing him. He sits down again.*

> [*After reading a few of the papers on his table*]: Your system won't get you anywhere.

ETIENNE: What system?

JUDGE: Your defence system. [*Pause.*] You lie too much. [*Pause. Aggressively.*] You were in the latrine with another man called Bruno, and you were manacled to him.

ETIENNE: But he was very ill, he didn't count.

JUDGE: Why did you escape on your own?

ETIENNE: I tell you, Bruno was very ill and he couldn't escape.

JUDGE: He didn't want to go with you?

ETIENNE: No, he couldn't have. He could hardly move. He was almost paralysed.

JUDGE [*interrupting him, shouts*]: Wait a minute.

> The JUDGE *makes a few notes with great care on a big sheet of white paper in gigantic handwriting. Holding the paper away from him he admires its effect with half-closed eyes.*

So he was paralysed then?

ETIENNE: Well, almost paralysed.

JUDGE: And he helped you run away?

ETIENNE: He couldn't.

JUDGE: Ah, of course not. But he didn't try to stop you, either?

ETIENNE: No, he didn't try to stop me.

JUDGE: And while you were filing through the chain you were hurting him.

ETIENNE: No, not at all.

JUDGE [*calmly*]: This business is going from bad to worse. [*Pause.*] Bruno wanted to escape but you didn't want to help him. On the other hand, he tried with all his might to stop you going, and what's more you hurt his ankles terribly while you were filing through the chain: he still bears the traces.

> The JUDGE *nibbles.* JUSTIN *is very pleased. The* JUDGE *drinks a mouthful of wine.*

Would you like us to go into the latrine and observe the traces?

ETIENNE: No.

JUDGE: You believe me, then?

ETIENNE: Yes.

JUDGE: You must have made poor Bruno suffer a lot.

JUSTIN [*getting up from his chair*]: Bruno isn't in the latrine. [*He sits down again.*]

JUDGE [*stopping his nibbling*]: Did you hear that?

ETIENNE: Yes.

JUDGE: Where is he, then?

ETIENNE: I've no idea.

JUDGE: You've no idea, and yet you were with him last. That's odd. Very odd.

ETIENNE: He must have escaped.

61

JUDGE: That's impossible. [*He looks for a paper on the table. He is holding in his hand a paper on which he has just written something.*] You've just told me that he could hardly move, that he was almost paralysed.

ETIENNE: He may have got better, though.

JUSTIN [*gets up again and speaks with great propriety. The* JUDGE *listens to him very attentively: he stops his nibbling*]: May I be permitted to inform you of certain facts which may throw some light on this case?

JUDGE: Please do.

JUSTIN: As you will have realised, your worship, the accused is adopting an attitude which might well deceive a tribunal that was inclined to be over-credulous. He is trying to make himself out an honourable man who is incapable of wrong-doing. Let us examine the facts with all the necessary accuracy: the accused was put in the latrine where he was chained to Bruno. He had been promised that he would be tried as soon as possible. But the accused, instead of quietly awaiting the day of his trial, forces the issue and escapes. Which can only be interpreted, purely and simply, as an inadmissible act of contempt of court. If the accused imagined that he was detained in the latrine for no reason, and even in a manner totally devoid of the most elementary courtesies as he gave us to understand at the beginning of the hearing, the only possible solution would have been for him to await the court's verdict, which is always in conformity with the law. I must stress this point: his lack of consideration towards the tribunal and his attempted escape must be interpreted as proof of his inadmissible attitude of contempt for the workings of justice and the law.

And now I have thrown some light on this first point, which may be considered as giving essential information about the attitude of the accused, I will pass on to others, of no less importance. The accused has admitted to having been lost in the park, to not knowing me, to having been chained to another person, etc. etc. That is to say that he has lied several times, and was trying, by his lies, to create the alibis necessary to conceal his wrong-doing. [*Pause.*] And I have been informed of some striking details by various people who, in these special circumstances, were witnesses to the events which took place in the latrine while the accused was confined there. The accused tortured Bruno with thirst; he was asking for water but the accused hardly ever took any notice. Then he had the idea of filing through the chain so that he could escape. The manacles were also secured round Bruno's ankles, since they were chained together, and the accused pulled so hard on Bruno's ankle that he made a deep wound. Bruno, overcome by pain and suffering, could do nothing to prevent the tortures the accused inflicted on him. The moment he was free he abandoned him without consideration for his thirst. [*Pause.*] But there is something even worse. [*Pause. Ceremonially.*] My servants have found Bruno's corpse in the park: he had been strangled. [*Pause.*] Although I am not aware of the precise details, I feel that all the circumstances prove that the accused strangled him.

ETIENNE [*violently*]: No. I didn't.

MICAELA *is distressed. The* JUDGE *starts eating again. He drinks a mouthful of wine and says in a calm voice.*

JUDGE: Well who did then? Are you going to accuse someone?

ETIENNE: He committed suicide.

JUDGE: How?

ETIENNE: With the lavatory chain.

JUDGE: You're contradicting yourself. You said at first that he could hardly move, that he was paralysed.

ETIENNE: He must have made a great effort.

JUSTIN: Don't forget that the body was found a long way from the latrine.

JUDGE: Yes. Can dead men walk?

ETIENNE *hesitates.*

ETIENNE: She and I [*pointing to* MICAELA] moved Bruno's body. We were afraid that if it was found I would be accused of murder.

JUSTIN [*very dignified*]: Your worship, I think it is useless to go any further. If the accused continues he will end by indicting us all. All the evidence points to his being the murderer, and as such he should be found guilty at once.

ETIENNE [*very angry*]: And who's he to talk about finding me guilty? He's the last one who can talk, he's the cruellest person I've ever met in all my life.

Silence. MICAELA *encourages* ETIENNE *and blows kisses at him.* JUSTIN *seems disconcerted. The* JUDGE *listens carefully.*

This man brought me into the park for no good reason and had me shut up in the middle of the labyrinth in a filthy lavatory with a kind of living corpse. And all this for no reason at all: out of sheer cruelty. And he's so cruel he ill-treats his daughter every day, and whips her. [*Ironical.*] Look at him, the good father, the father who loves his daughter. And in any case, Micaela isn't his daughter, and he often takes advantage of her, at the same time passing himself off as a good father, when he's nothing but a veritable tyrant. Look, look at Micaela's back, you'll see the traces of blood from the whip-lashes her father gave her last night.

JUSTIN [*to the* JUDGE]: May I ask you to verify the truth of what this man says?

JUDGE: There's no point.

JUSTIN: I should be grateful.

The JUDGE *bares* MICAELA'S *back. There's nothing wrong with it. It is white, and bears no trace of blood or scars.*

ETIENNE [*shouting*]: It's not possible.

MICAELA *covers her back.*

JUDGE: So that's how you behave to the man who came and got me out of bed so that you could be tried at once and not have to wait, the man who has done you nothing but kindnesses, and protected you from all sorts of dangers.

ETIENNE [*obstinately*]: He's a criminal. He can fake up anything he likes.

JUDGE: How dare you treat him like that? [*Pause.*] Actually, I'm nothing but his slave, he has the right of life and death over me. And anyway he appointed me to try you—and I have the reputation of being the most lenient judge of all on the emergency tribunal—simply to show you how much he has your interests at heart. I don't need to hear any more: the way you attack him and insult him is quite enough to prove your guilt.

JUSTIN: No—I want the trial to be based only on the observed actions of the accused from the time he entered the labyrinth, without any account being taken of what he has said against me.

JUDGE: You can certainly think yourself lucky.

The JUDGE *starts looking through his papers, and then goes on to others. Silence.*

There is not the slightest doubt of the accused's guilt.

He drinks a mouthful of wine. He nibbles a bit of sandwich.

The accused, from the very beginning of the hearing, has told all sorts of lies that it would be idle to recall; still worse, he has questioned the legal proceedings and attempted to escape. And to crown this series of offences, he has tortured his companion in the latrine, strangled him, and tried to dispose of his body in the park. The accused is found guilty of murder. [*Pause. He drinks. He nibbles.*] I condemn him to death. [*Pause. He drinks. He nibbles.*] The guards will come to fetch him at once, to the sound of the drum.

The JUDGE *stuffs all his papers in his pockets at record speed. The bottle, too. He attaches the chairs to the table, as they were to start with. While he is doing this* MICAELA *has gone over to her father and is stroking his back tenderly; from time to time her father kisses her on the forehead with great devotion.* ETIENNE *is crushed and stands there motionless.*

[*To* ETIENNE]: You are not to move from here. The guards will come and fetch you with their drums.

The JUDGE *goes out, pulling the table after him.* JUSTIN *and* MICAELA *follow him.* JUSTIN *tenderly supports his daughter, putting his arm round her shoulder. They go out.* ETIENNE *is left alone on the stage. Silence. Drums in the distance.* ETIENNE *looks anxiously towards the blankets. He hesitates. He goes into the labyrinth. Leaves the stage. Pause. The sound of the drums comes nearer.* ETIENNE *reappears, out of breath. The sound of the drums comes nearer.* ETIENNE *hesitates. He lifts up a blanket, intending to go into the labyrinth.* BRUNO *appears behind it, in his death throes.*

BRUNO: I'm thirsty.

ETIENNE *starts back in anguish. The blanket hides* BRUNO. *The drums come closer.* ETIENNE *hesitates. Very carefully he lifts up a blanket, intending to go into the labyrinth. There's no one there. He goes into the labyrinth. Leaves the stage. Pause. The sound of the drums comes nearer.* ETIENNE *reappears, out of breath. The sound of the drums comes nearer.* ETIENNE *hesitates. He lifts up a blanket, intending to go into the labyrinth.* BRUNO *appears behind it, in his death throes.*

BRUNO: I'm thirsty.

ETIENNE *starts back in anguish, the blanket hides* BRUNO, *the drums come nearer.* ETIENNE *hesitates, etc.*

CURTAIN

THE TRICYCLE

CHARACTERS

APAL
CLIMANDO
THE OLD FLUTE PLAYER
MITA
THE MAN WITH THE BANKNOTES
POLICEMAN
POLICE CHIEF

The action takes place on the banks of a river in a big town.

Iron rings along the quay. Path about 30 feet wide. Garden at the far end, separated from the path by a little wall, along the whole length of which runs a stone bench.

The Tricycle *was performed in Spanish in Madrid in 1957, under the direction of Josefina Sanchez-Pedreño, and premièred in France on February 15, 1961 in Paris, at the Théâtre de Poche Montparnasse, directed by Olivier Hussenot, with scenic design by Georges Richard.*

ACT ONE

Evening; it's not quite dark yet. APAL, *a poorly dressed individual, is lying on a bench.*

A VOICE: Apaaaal! . . . Apaaaal! . . . Apaaaal!

The voice is coming from the garden. Someone we can't see is crossing it, calling Apal. When he stops calling we can hear the tinkling of bells. The voice gradually dies away to nothing. Short silence. Then we again hear the voice and the bells.

THE VOICE: Apaaaal! . . . Apaaaal! . . . Apaaaal! . . .

The voice gets nearer and nearer, and CLIMANDO *finally enters, mounted on a rusty old box-tricycle. The box is decorated with characters from 'Alice in Wonderland' and is big enough to hold six children. It has a row of little bells on a crossbar.*

CLIMANDO [*getting down from the tricycle*]: Apal, Apal, wake up, mate.

He shakes him fairly roughly. APAL *wakes up and gets on to the tricycle, quickly, like an automaton.*

How come you aren't at the fountain?

APAL: I was sleepy.

APAL goes off on the tricycle. After a moment or two he comes back. He gets off the tricycle and lies down on the bench again.

CLIMANDO: But . . . aren't you going to the park, then?

APAL: I'm sleepy.

CLIMANDO: You've got a hell of a nerve.

APAL: Mmm . . .

CLIMANDO: And then, we've got to pay for the hire of the tricycle, and we haven't got a bean.

APAL: Let me sleep.

CLIMANDO: All right, all right. In any case you wouldn't have had much to do. Most of the kids have gone.

Enter the OLD FLUTE PLAYER.

OLD MAN: Hallo, boys! I'm going to sit down here, I don't feel I could walk another step.

CLIMANDO: That's just what I feel like too.

CLIMANDO *lies down by the river and the* OLD FLUTE PLAYER *sits down on the bench and stretches out his legs. Long pause.*

OLD MAN: It's because of the tricycle.

CLIMANDO: What is?

OLD MAN: Being so tired.

CLIMANDO: I'll say; I've spent the whole afternoon giving rides to kids. It hurts under my arms, more than anywhere else.

OLD MAN: It must be your espadrilles. Almost exactly the same thing happens to me; my knees hurt because I play the flute.

They both speak very quickly.

CLIMANDO: It must be your hat. Almost exactly the same thing happens to me; my nails hurt because I don't eat anything.

OLD MAN [*very cross*]: It must be the water you drink at the fountain. Almost exactly the same thing happens to me; my eyebrows hurt me because I wear trousers.

CLIMANDO [*aggressive*]: It must be your not being married. Almost exactly the same thing happens to me; the flies hurt me because I go to sleep.

OLD MAN [*violently*]: It must be your not buying lottery tickets. Almost exactly the same thing happens to me; all the hairs on my head hurt because I walk.

CLIMANDO [*very pleased*]: It's not true. It's not true!

OLD MAN: It's not true?

CLIMANDO: No, no, it's not true; all the hairs on your head can't possibly hurt you because you're bald.

OLD MAN: You're cheating.

CLIMANDO: No I'm not; we'll start again if you like.

OLD MAN: We can't; you reason better than I do, and reason always wins.

CLIMANDO: You won't go about saying I took unfair advantage of you, will you? I'll give you a ride on the tricycle, if you like.

OLD MAN [*relenting*]: A ride on the tricycle! And will you let me stroke the children?

CLIMANDO: Yes—so long as you don't steal their chocolate.

OLD MAN: You see how you dislike me? What's their chocolate got to do with it? You see? Eh?

CLIMANDO *is ashamed.*

Don't hang your head—don't. [*Pleased.*] So you do realise how badly you treat me, eh?

CLIMANDO [*humbly*]: Yes. [*Justifying himself.*] But I did promise to give you a ride on the tricycle. I can't be any nicer than that.

OLD MAN [*softly*]: A ride on the tricycle . . . stroking the children. I'll put my hands on their heads and say . . . and say . . . [*aggressively*] Yes, but will you let me play the bells?

CLIMANDO: No, because you have to play the flute, and no one's ever been known to play two instruments at the same time.

OLD MAN: You won't let me because I haven't got any banknotes and I'm not good at reasoning. Goodbye! [*He goes off angrily as far as the end of the bench, and turns his back on* CLIMANDO.] And afterwards you won't say *pax*, or give me a sardine . . . or bring me a mouthful of water when I'm thirsty.

CLIMANDO: You take me for Father Christmas.

CLIMANDO *sits down by the river and starts fishing. He throws a baited line into the water.*

CLIMANDO [*intoning, making each syllable very clear and detached*]: And then, Apal and I are going to be very pleased with ourselves because we've thought up a marvellous scheme. We shan't let anyone else into the secret.

71

OLD MAN [*also intoning*]: I'm going to be very pleased with myself on account of a different scheme. I shan't say a word to anyone, just to rile the idiots who won't let me have a ride on the tricycle.

Pause.

CLIMANDO: We've discovered a way to stop anyone following us, so's we don't have to escape from one place to another, like we do now.

OLD MAN: I'd be mighty surprised if Apal had done something.

APAL *wakes up for the second time. He runs round the stage twice. Then he starts slapping himself on the back, crossing his arms.*

[*Going off*]: Right, I'm off.

CLIMANDO [*to* APAL, *without looking at him*]: Are you cold?

APAL: Yes.

CLIMANDO: If you like, we'll go and sleep by the metro.

APAL: There's the cops. [*He always speaks as if it's a great effort.*]

CLIMANDO: That's true. Yes, but we could go and sleep near the kitchens of the Grand Hotel.

APAL: The porter.

CLIMANDO: Yes, that porter fellow doesn't care for us overmuch; the old goat chucks water over us. [*Pause.*] We could sneak into a cinema.

APAL: Very difficult.

CLIMANDO: And all because we aren't invisible. Ah! if only we were invisible! Apal, if I were invisible, I'd go and sleep in a box in the Green Palace. On the carpet! I'd be all right there! But what can we do to find somewhere warm to sleep?

APAL: Die!

CLIMANDO: Die?

APAL: We haven't got any money, so we'd go to hell.

CLIMANDO: But the thing is, I'm afraid.

APAL: So'm I.

CLIMANDO: We're not so poor as all that. We've got the tricycle. [*Pause.*] The trouble is that if we don't pay for its hire tomorrow they'll take it back. And we haven't got anything else.

APAL: We've been worse off before.

CLIMANDO: The worst of all is the cold. There's one thing we can do. We can sleep together, and when you say: 'Climando, my feet are cold,' I'll blow on them for you. And when I say: 'Apal, my hands are cold,' you can blow on my hands for me.

APAL: That's tiring.

CLIMANDO: No more than lifting your little finger.

APAL: I'm going to have a snooze.

CLIMANDO: You do nothing else all day.

> CLIMANDO *sits down by the river bank and whistles as he casts a line into the water in an attempt to catch some fish. Enter* MITA, *a young girl dressed in black rags.*

Hi, Mita!

MITA: Hi! [*She sits down near* CLIMANDO.]

CLIMANDO: You're terribly sad!

> MITA *makes a vague gesture.*

I ought to give you a kiss so's you won't be sad. [*Pause.*] I like your kisses better than the ovens in the patisserie in the avenue.

MITA: That's more or less how it is with me, about you. But we can't make a meal out of kisses.

CLIMANDO: Then you like cakes better than my kisses.

MITA: 'Course I do!

CLIMANDO: Well, I do too.

MITA: We're awfully alike.

CLIMANDO: We were born for each other. [*Gaily.*] We both like cakes better than kisses.

MITA: But I'm very sad.

CLIMANDO: What's happened?

MITA: Nothing.

CLIMANDO: Really nothing?

MITA: Yes, really, really nothing.

CLIMANDO: Oh my goodness, you must be sad!

MITA: I'd like to commit suicide, I'm so sad.

CLIMANDO: Really and truly?

73

MITA: Yes.

CLIMANDO: Why?

MITA: I don't know—no reason. Then I wouldn't be sad any more.

CLIMANDO: Oh, that's true, nor you would. I hadn't thought of that.

MITA: If only I had the courage!

CLIMANDO [*after a long moment's meditation*]: It's obvious. Commit suicide.

MITA: It's the best thing to do, don't you think?

CLIMANDO: Of course it's the best thing to do. I see it now. I was going to be sorry about it because I like you a lot— more than the tricycle—and then your kisses are almost better than anchovy sandwiches. But Mita, if you think you'll be happier committing suicide, commit suicide as soon as possible.

MITA: You're so good! You give me such good advice!

CLIMANDO: There's no doubt about it—you, and the old flute man, even though he is such a cross-patch, and Apal, are what I love most in the world. Commit suicide, Mita, don't be afraid.

MITA: Why don't you, too?

CLIMANDO: Well, I hadn't thought about it. And anyway, I've got to pay for the hire of the tricycle tomorrow. I can't commit suicide. Tell Apal, in case he wants to commit suicide too.

MITA: Not Apal. He's always asleep.

CLIMANDO: Tell the old man, then.

MITA: He's very old to think about suicide.

CLIMANDO: That's true, it's never happened yet. That'd be bad.

MITA: And anyway, he could only commit suicide with his flute; just think how ugly and difficult that'd be.

CLIMANDO: Yes, but he could climb on to a roof, though, and hide his eyes, and then just when he was least expecting it—woomph—and he'd be dead.

MITA: But what if he doesn't get giddy? When you're old you don't even get giddy any more.

74

CLIMANDO: That's a nuisance. [*Pause.*] And how are *you* going to commit suicide?

MITA: I've forgotten.

CLIMANDO: You always forget everything. Do you remember the day when you were walking down a little street arm in arm with Apal and you met a bus driver and said to him: 'Hey, don't go away, it's my birthday tomorrow,' and he didn't listen to you and went away?

MITA: That doesn't mean I forget everything.

CLIMANDO: Hm! Nor it does! [*Pause.*] The trouble is that when you've committed suicide I won't be able to stroke your knees.

MITA: You can stroke Cepina's—you know, the girl who sells pancakes.

CLIMANDO: And what is there to tell me that her knees are as pretty as yours?

MITA: I know my knees are pretty but hers aren't bad either. She washes them every morning with water and herbs.

CLIMANDO: They won't be like yours, I tell you . . . let me stroke them again.

> MITA *raises her skirts a little and* CLIMANDO *strokes her knees.*

I love your knees because they're soft, and smooth, and big and white, like a china plate only more velvety. And then they aren't wrinkled like mine. I'll show you how ugly they are.

> CLIMANDO *starts to take off one of his boots.*

MITA: Why do you take off your boot to show me your knee?

CLIMANDO: Er . . . my trouser leg has to be in my boot, you see, so I don't catch cold. [*He finally manages to take off his boots, and pulls his trousers up to his knees.*] Look—touch them, touch them and you'll see.

MITA [*touching them*]: Pooh! Aren't they ugly, aren't they wrinkled!

CLIMANDO: And what's more, you're seeing them on a day when I've eaten some bread soaked in tunny fish oil. You just ought to see them the other days.

MITA: And then, they're very dirty.

CLIMANDO: That's because I don't wash them.

MITA: Ah!

APAL *moves, probably trying to find a more comfortable position.*

CLIMANDO: Apal, when on earth are you going to stop sleeping?

APAL: Mmm. . . .

MITA: Leave him, Climando, you know very well he has to sleep at least 18 hours a day.

CLIMANDO: Yes, but one of these days he'll die from sleeping so much.

MITA: That doesn't worry him in the slightest. His dreams must be much sweeter.

CLIMANDO: I'm sure he's dreaming that he's asleep.

MITA: That must be very pleasant.

CLIMANDO: Wonderful! And then, when he's awake, as he never does anything, he can't be any happier. We're much less happy than he is, we're always having to hide from the cops, and porters, and men with money. And worst of all is the fact that we haven't got any means of paying for the hire of the tricycle. [*Pause.*] They'll put us in prison.

MITA: In prison—that won't be much fun. They say they're full of bugs, and the worst thing is that they keep on having hunger strikes, so that if you don't look out you die.

CLIMANDO: You needn't bother about that. The tricycle isn't yours. . . . And anyway, you're going to commit suicide.

MITA: I'd forgotten all about it.

CLIMANDO: You see how you forget everything.

MITA: I'd only forgotten I was supposed to commit suicide.

CLIMANDO: And you needn't think I'm joking. That's how people start. For instance—I had a friend who wore braces on Sundays and a belt on every other day, and that's why he drank more than usual on Sundays.

MITA: Yes, of course. But what do I have to do to remember I've got to commit suicide?

CLIMANDO: Make a note of it, or else tie a knot in your handkerchief.

MITA: . . .

CLIMANDO: It's in your own interests. Just think that you won't be happy unless you commit suicide.

MITA: Really?

CLIMANDO: Of course. So you see—commit suicide as soon as possible.

MITA: And won't you be sorry?

CLIMANDO [*tenderly*]: Me, Mita? Yes, very, terribly. I love you so much. You and your kisses, your white, smooth, big knees.

MITA: I love you too, even though you're so incredibly ugly.

CLIMANDO: I'll let you take the tricycle back to the garage if you like, Mita.

MITA: Will you really?

    CLIMANDO *nods happily*.

What a bit of luck! [*Pause.*] And will you let me steer it with one hand?

CLIMANDO: Only one hand? [*He considers.*] Well, all right. [*He considers.*] And what'll you do with the other?

MITA: I'll put one of my fingers up my nose.

CLIMANDO: You are a one! You can do everything.

MITA [*enthusiastically*]: If you like I'll even steer with my eyes shut.

CLIMANDO: Oh no you don't. You'd fall in the water and the fishes would eat you.

MITA [*terrified*]: Oh my goodness!

CLIMANDO: You have to be told everything. What would become of you if I wasn't here?

MITA: All right. I'll take the tricycle back to the garage without shutting my eyes.

CLIMANDO: And come straight back. The garage is no distance, it'll only take you two minutes.

MITA: Don't worry.

CLIMANDO: And don't play about behind the trees watching the men peeing.

MITA: No, you'll see, I'll come straight back. See you.

CLIMANDO: See you.

> MITA *gets on to the tricycle and goes off. The bells can be heard.* CLIMANDO *hesitates. He walks up and down, thinking. He goes over to* APAL *and shakes him to wake him up.*

Apal, you've had your 18 hours.

APAL: Mmm. . . .

CLIMANDO: Come on Apal, wake up.

APAL: Mmm. . . .

CLIMANDO: You're just like a dormouse! Come on, chum, get up, wake up.

> APAL *slowly sits up.*

APAL: What's going on?

CLIMANDO: We've got to find the money for the hire of the tricycle.

APAL: Where?

CLIMANDO: That's just what I don't know.

APAL: Doesn't matter.

CLIMANDO: But they'll put us in prison.

APAL: Well, they can.

CLIMANDO: And they'll take the tricycle away from us.

APAL: Well, they can.

CLIMANDO: But what'll we do, you and I?

APAL: *I* shall sleep.

CLIMANDO: We must think of something.

APAL: Personally what I must do is sleep. When I think, I'm hungry and cold.

CLIMANDO: Yes, that's the trouble with thinking.

APAL: Especially if the things you think about are very worrying.

CLIMANDO: Why don't you tell yourself some nice stories?

APAL: I don't know.

CLIMANDO: That's very bad. [*Pause.*] And you can't think of any way of paying for the tricycle?

APAL: No.

> *Enter* MITA. APAL *takes advantage of her arrival to go to sleep.*

78

MITA [*to* CLIMANDO]: Look.

She points to someone we can't see on her right.

CLIMANDO: What a peculiar-looking chap! What's he doing here?

MITA: He's following me. *He* must like my knees, too.

CLIMANDO: No, not he. He looks peculiar: people like that don't like your knees.

MITA: But he's following me.

CLIMANDO: Don't be afraid. He won't dare take us both on. In any case, if he does, we'll call Apal to help us.

MITA: Can't you see he's asleep?

CLIMANDO: We'll wake him up.

MITA: Yes, we'd better.

CLIMANDO [*looking to the right*]: He's stopped.

MITA [*pointing to him*]: He's looking at us.

CLIMANDO: Did he say anything to you?

MITA: No, he just showed me his wallet.

CLIMANDO: Were there many notes in it?

MITA: It was full.

CLIMANDO: Then why's he following you? Greedy pig! The more you have the more you want. Just imagine, he not only has a wallet full of banknotes but he wants you, too.

MITA: Yes, he's going a bit far.

CLIMANDO: Well, I don't think much of his taste, considering how dirty you are today.

MITA: That's true—I *am* very dirty.

CLIMANDO: And he can't like you. He doesn't know your good sides. He can't know that you can walk in a barrel, or that you can draw in the sand with your toes, or that you make paper boats. So as he doesn't know anything about all that, he can't like you.

MITA: No, of course he can't.

CLIMANDO: Peculiar chap. [*Long pause.*] Don't you remember—I knew you when you were pulling posters off the walls to sell the paper. He'll never know such joy with you. I carried the bag half way to Sarpe's shop and you carried it the rest of the way. And afterwards we used the money to buy peanuts from old Simplicie. What does he want?

If he has so many banknotes all he has to do is buy
enough peanuts to make him sick and then he'll be
quite happy.

MITA: The trouble is that men who have banknotes wear
very ugly suits and shave a lot, that's why their faces look
like bits of silk. It's disgusting. And they can't breathe
properly, which is even worse. And they're always getting
tired. It's nauseating. If I had a lot of money I'd wear the
same clothes as I do now and I'd eat lots of sardine sandwiches, and when the nights were cold I'd spend them in the
warm, but in the summer I'd come and sleep by the river.

CLIMANDO: That's what you say now, but if you had a lot of
money one day you'd only buy silly and ugly things which
aren't any use.

MITA: Quite likely.

CLIMANDO: There's not the slightest doubt. People make a
lot of promises and then they get rich and forget all about
them. That little Vincent, for instance, Moscona's son—
he got pneumonia when he was five months old and then
when he was six years he fell downstairs.

MITA: Misfortunes seldom come singly.

CLIMANDO: The worst misfortune is to die of hunger, and
hunger always comes by itself.

MITA: Huh! So it does.

CLIMANDO: That's why, when I die, I want them to throw my
fishing line into the water for the fishes to eat, and I want
the old flute player to play a sad or gay tune while they do it.

MITA [looking to the right]: Hey, d'you see how he's looking
at us?

CLIMANDO: He is too. He must be a low type.

MITA: Does he think he's going to stay there all night?

CLIMANDO: People like him are very annoying. You'd think
they'd nothing better to do. [Pause.] I feel almost sorry
for him.

MITA: Yes of course, poor chap.

CLIMANDO: Naturally—poor chap. And all because he wants
to kiss you, probably. [He stares at her.] Don't be nasty to
him.

MITA [*touched*]: He's sad.

CLIMANDO: Yes, he is. And it's all your fault. Don't you feel sorry for him?

MITA: Yes, very sorry. But he's horribly ugly.

CLIMANDO: Then you ought to feel even sorrier for him.

MITA: Yes, but I feel even more disgusted.

CLIMANDO: Think it's me. If you shut your eyes you won't be able to tell the difference.

MITA: Won't I?

CLIMANDO: 'Course you won't.

MITA: But he's got some banknotes.

CLIMANDO: So he has; I'd forgotten.

MITA: If he's got some banknotes it'll be all the same to him whether he kisses me or someone else. You can buy what you like when you've got money, you can even buy a thousand tins of anchovies.

CLIMANDO: I've got an idea. Why couldn't we take the notes he's got in his wallet?

MITA: And what'd we do with so much money?

CLIMANDO: We'd take what we need to pay for the hire of the tricycle.

MITA: Is that all?

CLIMANDO: We could take enough to buy four sandwiches, too—one for Apal, one for the old man, one for you, and one for me.

MITA: And a brazier, too.

CLIMANDO: And . . . [*annoyed*] We can't ask for anything else or we'd get to be like tortoises.

MITA: That's the trouble, when you ask for things.

CLIMANDO: Yes but—how can we take the banknotes?

MITA: I don't know. You ought to know better than I do, you're a man.

CLIMANDO: I could say: 'Beg your pardon, sir, but what colour is your wallet?' And he'd say: 'Green', and I'd say: 'Red' until he has to take it out to prove it. And then we'd grab it and run away. As he's a rich man, either he won't be able to run or else he'll run like a duck and he'll never be able to catch us.

81

MITA: But what if his wallet is red?

CLIMANDO: Yes, then it's more serious.

MITA: We've got to think of everything.

CLIMANDO: Best thing would be to ask Apal what he thinks.

MITA: Yes, that'd be best.

CLIMANDO: Apal, Apal, Apal.[*He shakes him.*] You've had your 18 hours.

APAL: Mmm. . . .

CLIMANDO: Come on, Apal, wake up.

    APAL *sits up.*

APAL: What is it?

CLIMANDO [*pointing*]: You see that chap?

APAL: Yes.

CLIMANDO: He's got a lot of banknotes.

APAL: Good.

CLIMANDO: We've got to take them from him to pay for the hire of the tricycle.

APAL: Mmm. . . .

CLIMANDO: How can we take them?

APAL: I don't know.

CLIMANDO: Can't you think of anything? Try really hard, like when you're looking for somewhere to sleep.

APAL [*after a pause*]. By killing him.

CLIMANDO: By killing him?

MITA: That's going too far.

CLIMANDO [*looking* MITA *in the eyes*]: Don't say you're scared. Or are you suddenly going to discover that you're superstitious, or that you're afraid of the dead? You wanted to commit suicide.

MITA: That's different.

CLIMANDO: You needn't think it's so very different. It's a question of death in both cases, when you really come down to it.

MITA: But in one case it was *my* death.

CLIMANDO: Even worse. I remember so well the day I fell downstairs.

MITA: Apal's going off to sleep again.

CLIMANDO: Apal—how do we kill him?

APAL: Very simple.

MITA: Of course—couldn't be more simple, there are three of us.

CLIMANDO: I don't very much like having to kill him. It's a terribly long way of robbing him.

MITA: It's the only way for no one to know. If we don't kill him the first thing he'll do is go and ask the judge to lock us up, and as he's sure to have some more banknotes at home he can do what he likes.

CLIMANDO: What a rotten sort of chap.

MITA: And anyway, he's sure to want to commit suicide.

CLIMANDO: I hadn't thought of that.

MITA: We'll be saving him the trouble.

CLIMANDO [*to* APAL]: Don't go to sleep now, mate.

APAL: I'm listening.

CLIMANDO: We agree; we'll kill him.

APAL: Good.

CLIMANDO: But how?

APAL [*pointing to the garden wall*]: Over there.

CLIMANDO: Do we throw ourselves on him?

APAL: Yes: Mita must stay here to attract his attention.

> CLIMANDO *and* APAL *start to go off.*

MITA: I'm scared.

CLIMANDO: Don't be daft, think about the tricycle and the anchovy sandwiches, and about how he wants to commit suicide. Don't move, don't move.

> *He retreats, step by step, towards the wings, saying in a sing-song voice:*

Don't move, watch for the birdie. Don't move.

> MITA *is left alone on the stage. She starts humming, to keep up her courage, and then pulls up the rags that cover her knees. Her voice becomes more and more assured as she sings. The man with the banknotes comes in slowly. Before he gets to* MITA *the lights gradually dim until there is complete darkness.*

CURTAIN

ACT TWO

MITA *can be heard singing. Then a short silence. The lights gradually come up again.* APAL *is back on the bench, asleep. The bench is covered with blood stains. Enter the* OLD FLUTE PLAYER.

OLD MAN: Hey, Apal, have you seen that? [*He points to the stains.*] What a mess! [*He follows the bloodstains and smells them.*] Someone must have killed an animal here, don't you think? [*Pause.*] Unless it was an elephant . . . What a lot of blood!

APAL [*without getting up*]: What's going on?

OLD MAN: Look, there's blood all over the place.

APAL: Don't disturb me.

OLD MAN: But my dear chap, can't you see all the blood?

APAL: Yes, of course I can.

OLD MAN: We must do something.

APAL: Leave me alone, I'm sleepy.

OLD MAN: Well you are a one! Right, I'm off, I don't want to know anything about it. Blood makes me thirsty and the water's very cold at the moment, and wine's very dear. Goodbye, Apal.

APAL: Mmm. . . .

The OLD FLUTE PLAYER *goes off.* APAL *runs round the stage twice, trying not to tread in the blood. Then he slaps himself on the back and lies down again. Silence. We hear the tricycle bells tinkling. Then* MITA *and* CLIMANDO *come in, riding on the tricycle.*

CLIMANDO [*loudly and happily*]: Apal, Apal, I've paid for the hire of the tricycle.

APAL: Aren't you going to let me sleep?

MITA: Of course we are; let him sleep, Climando, he did a lot of work yesterday.

CLIMANDO: So he did.

MITA: People always think it's dead easy to kill someone.

CLIMANDO: Personally I think he might have found somewhere else to sleep.

MITA: No, because blood's lucky.

CLIMANDO: No, it's salt that's lucky.

MITA: No no, I remember perfectly—blood on the ground brings luck to the chickens.

CLIMANDO: But Apal isn't a chicken.

MITA: It's a saying.

CLIMANDO: Oh.

MITA: We haven't given him the sandwich.

CLIMANDO: Nor we have.

MITA: Call him.

CLIMANDO: Apal, Apal!

APAL: What is it?

CLIMANDO: We've brought you a sandwich.

APAL: Thanks. [APAL *eats it*.]

CLIMANDO: Is it good?

APAL: Yes.

CLIMANDO: It didn't cost much.

APAL: That's good.

CLIMANDO: We've still got ten notes left.

MITA: And we've paid for the hire of the tricycle.

CLIMANDO: Now we'll be able to live in peace.

APAL: Maybe.

Enter the OLD FLUTE PLAYER.

OLD MAN: There's a lot of cops over there.

He points to his right.

CLIMANDO: Why?

OLD MAN: I don't know.

CLIMANDO: Perhaps there's a procession.

OLD MAN: No, because they have tanks in processions.

CLIMANDO: But you *can* have a procession without tanks.

OLD MAN: Not possible. They need tanks to make the ground level.

CLIMANDO: No, to level the ground in processions they have flags.

OLD MAN: Never, they have flags to hide the tall soldiers.

CLIMANDO: The tall ones wear short coats so's they don't look so tall.

OLD MAN: That's not right, either. They give short coats to the soldiers who haven't got any hair on their legs.

CLIMANDO: It's not true, it's not true. Soldiers who haven't got any hair on their legs aren't soldiers. They're soldieresses. And as there aren't any soldieresses, what you're saying isn't true.

OLD MAN: You're cheating again.

CLIMANDO: We'll start again if you like.

OLD MAN: No, because you reason better than I do and reason always wins.

CLIMANDO: You always say that but the truth is you're afraid and you're trying to find excuses for yourself.

OLD MAN: They're not excuses, they're truths. You cheat all the time.

CLIMANDO: No, no, no and no. Do you remember the fountain in the rue du Peigne? Yes—well, that fountain was flooded the other day when a hay cart fell into it.

OLD MAN: You just say that to impress me. But you know very well you're cheating.

CLIMANDO: I'll give you something to make up for it if you like.

OLD MAN: What?

CLIMANDO: Well um . . . um . . . um . . . [Silence.] Well . . . I don't know.

OLD MAN: You see—you don't want to give me anything. You see how you immediately climb down? You see how you dislike me? You see?

CLIMANDO is ashamed.

Don't hang your head—don't. [Pleased.] So you do realise now that you cheat and that you treat me terribly badly, do you? Tell me—do you realise?

CLIMANDO [very humbly]: Yes, I do.

OLD MAN: I knew it.

CLIMANDO [*becoming natural again*]: But I'd promised to give you something to make up for it . . . I know what I'll give you. I'll cut out two letters from every word you say.

OLD MAN: Two letters? [*The* OLD MAN *thinks for a few moments. Delighted.*] Two letters, eh? What about in the word *it*? And in the word *A*? And in the word SSS? And in the word TTT? And in the word ddd? And in the word ggg? And in the word E? And in the word fff? And worst of all, in the word . . .?

No sound can be heard.

CLIMANDO: Which one?

OLD MAN: In the word . . . [*He looks as if he's saying something but no sound can be heard.*]

CLIMANDO: Which one?

MITA: Can't you hear it's the h in honour?

CLIMANDO: Oh!

OLD MAN: What've you got to say to that, eh? You were trying to cheat again. What were you thinking, eh? Answer me!

CLIMANDO: That you're older, and that as you'll die before I do, you're better at this sort of discussion than I am. Now you'll be able to win. But the most important thing is that you have a lot more experience than I have.

MITA: But you both argue very badly. As if you were half-fare passengers.

CLIMANDO: You keep out of this.

OLD MAN: You women, all you can do is make sewing machines.

They are speaking very fast, and shouting.

CLIMANDO: And forks.

OLD MAN: Those, and forks, that's all you can produce.

CLIMANDO: And keys.

OLD MAN: Those, and keys, that's all you can produce.

CLIMANDO: And children that look like horses.

OLD MAN: Those, and children that look like horses. That's all you can produce.

CLIMANDO: And ashtrays.

OLD MAN: And ashtrays, that's right, that's all.

CLIMANDO: And wars.
OLD MAN: Those, and wars.
CLIMANDO: And blankets.
OLD MAN: Those, and blankets.
CLIMANDO: And weddings.
OLD MAN: Those, and weddings.
CLIMANDO: And ties.
OLD MAN: Those, and ties.
CLIMANDO: And emperors.
OLD MAN: Those, and emperors.
CLIMANDO: And lavatories.
OLD MAN: Those, and lavatories.
CLIMANDO: And banknotes.
OLD MAN: Those, and banknotes.
CLIMANDO: And banknotes.
OLD MAN: And banknotes.
CLIMANDO: And banknotes.
OLD MAN: And banknotes.
CLIMANDO: And banknotes.
OLD MAN: And banknotes.
CLIMANDO: And banknotes.
OLD MAN: And banknotes.

> *They go on saying* 'and banknotes' *till they fall to the ground, exhausted.*

MITA: Of course, now you'll be able to boast of knowing how to conduct an argument.
OLD MAN [*trying to get up*]: She' . . . s . . .won.
MITA: Come on, pull yourselves together.
OLD MAN [*still on the ground*]: We . . . we . . . can't.

> MITA *brings her lips close to the old man's. Both he and* CLIMANDO *then make an effort and raise their hesitating heads to her. But* MITA *moves away. They fall back in despair. This is repeated several times.*

Lea . . .ve . . . us . . . a . . . lone . . . Mi . . . ta . . .
MITA [*sitting down on the bench*]: Come on, jump to it—last person up pays a forfeit.

CLIMANDO *and the* OLD FLUTE PLAYER *make a great effort and stand up*.

CLIMANDO [*in an imploring voice*]: Mita, why do you treat us so badly? What have we done to you? Mita, I love you very much.

OLD MAN: So do I—I love you too.

MITA: So do I—I love you both very much.

CLIMANDO: And Apal loves you, too.

OLD MAN: And so do the cops.

MITA: And so do I—I love Apal and the cops.

CLIMANDO: The cops?

MITA: Yes, the cops.

CLIMANDO: But what are they doing, the cops?

MITA: They're having a procession.

CLIMANDO [*to the* OLD MAN]: Go and see what the cops are doing.

OLD MAN: What'll you give me?

CLIMANDO: Nothing.

OLD MAN: Right: so long.

He goes out.

MITA: Aren't you going to the park today, to give rides to the kids?

CLIMANDO: No, it's not a holiday today.

MITA: If things go on like this you'll never have any money.

CLIMANDO: But I'll have lots of sun, and lots of sand to make castles with, and lots of leaves on the trees.

MITA: But you'll never be able to buy a potted plant.

CLIMANDO: What *I* like is sugar lumps. So white and so hard.

The OLD MAN *comes in, running.*

OLD MAN [*speaking very quickly*]: The cops are coming for you.

CLIMANDO: Us?

OLD MAN [*pointing to* APAL]: They're looking for you—you and Apal. They say you've got to stay here quietly until the chief comes.

CLIMANDO: Why?

MITA: You never listen to the cops.

CLIMANDO: But I never understand them.

90

MITA: Well—make an effort, then. I don't understand them either, and when I see one in one street I go down another. Yesterday, for instance, I was just picking up some papers when I suddenly saw an apple—well, I didn't waste a minute, I ate it. Not you, though. When you see a cop it doesn't make any difference to you either way, he's just like one of the family.

CLIMANDO: It's a habit.

MITA: And what a habit! Don't think that's any excuse.

OLD MAN: Of course it isn't.

CLIMANDO: But I behave nicely.

OLD MAN [sing-song]: Yes yes, you do. [In his normal voice.] And the way you cheat—what've you got to say about that?

CLIMANDO: Quite true. But I don't cheat to annoy you. If I wanted to annoy you I could pour water over your head when you're asleep, for instance.

OLD MAN: Yes yes, I agree—that would be more annoying.

MITA: But then, what have you done wrong? Try and remember.

CLIMANDO [counting on his fingers]: That business with the cops, cheating the old man, the time I . . . [Silence.] I can't think of anything else.

MITA: Make an effort, mate.

CLIMANDO: Ah! I remember. One day . . . [He stops. Silence.]

MITA: What?

OLD MAN: Go on—what? What?

MITA: Come on, be brave, Climando.

CLIMANDO: Well, one day . . .

   The other two punctuate his words with nods.

. . . but that made me very sad.

MITA: Oh no, you mustn't let that make you sad.

OLD MAN: Now he claims to be sad. You—sad?

MITA: Well, yes, it could have made him sad.

OLD MAN: Don't you believe it. There's no reason. Does he like corn, by any chance? No—well then, how could he be sad?

MITA: He might, though—it could have made him sad. But who knows whether he writes with both hands?

OLD MAN: No one. Absolutely no one can know. Not even his own shoe. That's asking too much of us.

MITA: The thing is, you don't like Climando.

OLD MAN: Oh yes I do—very much.

MITA: Well, what have we decided? Does Climando make you sad or doesn't he?

OLD MAN: He does—very.

MITA [to CLIMANDO]: Climando, you make us very sad.

CLIMANDO [with tears in his eyes]: I make myself even sadder than I do you.

OLD MAN: Why?

CLIMANDO: I've forgotten.

OLD MAN: You've forgotten?

CLIMANDO: Yes, I've forgotten, d'you think I can't forget the things that make me sad?

OLD MAN: Of course.

MITA: But what *we* wanted to know was why the cops are looking for you.

CLIMANDO: Who?

OLD MAN: Apal and you.

CLIMANDO: Apal and me?

OLD MAN: Yes.

MITA: Yes.

CLIMANDO [calling] Apal, Apal.

APAL: Hmm. . . .

CLIMANDO: Apal, wake up, you've had your 18 hours.

APAL: What's going on?

CLIMANDO: The cops are looking for us.

APAL: Why?

CLIMANDO: I don't know. Don't *you* know?

APAL: Yes.

CLIMANDO: Why?

APAL: For the murder of the man with the banknotes.

MITA: Of course that's why.

CLIMANDO: But Apal, we haven't ever slept in the warm since then.

APAL: No.

CLIMANDO: And anyway, we didn't mean any harm when we killed him.

OLD MAN: And where's it all written down?

MITA: That's right, it has to be in writing.

OLD MAN: And signed by the most important chief in the district.

CLIMANDO: I haven't asked him.

MITA: He hasn't had time.

OLD MAN: And what d'you think's going to happen? That everything's going to fall into your lap?

CLIMANDO: But he wanted to commit suicide.

OLD MAN: The document.

MITA: You're sure to need to put that in writing, too.

CLIMANDO: I can say I've left it at home.

OLD MAN: They're not idiots, you know.

MITA: Well . . . idiots. There's nothing in the least idiotic about them. I've heard that they've got carriages that can go even faster than two horses galloping their fastest.

APAL: We killed him.

CLIMANDO: But it was the first time.

MITA [*to the old man*]: How many times do you have to do it before it's wrong?

OLD MAN: Once is enough.

MITA: And twice?

OLD MAN: That's enough, too.

MITA: And three times?

OLD MAN: I haven't got as far as that, I only know the first two by heart.

CLIMANDO [*to* APAL]: Apal—but we're good, we don't want to go to war.

APAL: Maybe.

CLIMANDO: We don't walk on the grass, either.

APAL: Pooh!

CLIMANDO: And we don't steal the kids' chocolate, either.

APAL: That doesn't help.

CLIMANDO: And when I had a stomach ache you didn't sleep, so's you could look after me.

APAL: That's not important.

93

CLIMANDO: What shall we do, Apal?

APAL: Sleep.

    APAL *lies down. Long pause.*

CLIMANDO: Don't go to sleep, Apal, they're coming to get us.

APAL: They'll wake us up all right.

CLIMANDO [*to the* OLD MAN]: What did they tell you, the cops?

OLD MAN: I've already told you.

CLIMANDO: Yes, but I've forgotten.

MITA [*sing-song voice*]: I thought I was the only one who forgot things.

CLIMANDO: It must be catching.

MITA: Well, tie a knot in your handkerchief, then.

CLIMANDO: Will that stop it being catching?

MITA: I don't remember whether that stops it being catching or whether it helps you to remember.

CLIMANDO: No one's ever taught me anything of that sort.

MITA: Of course not; all anyone ever taught you was to ride a tricycle.

CLIMANDO: It's a profession. Everyone says that a profession is the best thing you can have.

MITA: It's better to have a lot of money.

CLIMANDO: It's even better to be able to swing from branch to branch without ever falling once.

MITA: It's better still to have a thousand aeroplanes.

CLIMANDO: It's better to be able to swim underwater and not come up to the surface for 45 hours.

MITA: It's much better to have a thousand submarines.

CLIMANDO: It's better to sing all day long from the top of a tree.

MITA: It's much better to have a thousand records.

CLIMANDO: You only say all that because you don't like my having learnt to be a professional tricycle driver.

OLD MAN [*tenderly*]: Tricycle driver! Isn't that pretty! It's much prettier than playing the flute.

MITA: There's more to a tricycle than to a flute because you use your feet, too.

OLD MAN: When I have some money I shall buy myself a

tricycle and take the kids for rides in the park and stroke . their heads.

CLIMANDO: And pinch their chocolate. I can see it all.

OLD MAN: You're picking on me again. You see?

MITA: Yes, Climando, you really are picking on him. Ask him to forgive you, at once.

OLD MAN [*pleased*]: That's it, that's it, let him ask me to forgive him.

MITA: Come on, Climando, ask him to forgive you.

CLIMANDO: Please forgive me. [*He adds, under his breath.*] With my fingers crossed.

OLD MAN: What did you say?

CLIMANDO: Well—please forgive me . . . [*After a very short pause, he adds.*] With my fingers crossed.

OLD MAN: What d'you say?

CLIMANDO: What d'you think I'm saying? Please forgive me . . . [*Pause.*] My fingers crossed.

OLD MAN [*open-eyed*]: With your fingers crossed?

MITA: Yes, he said he had his fingers crossed.

CLIMANDO: It's two to one, you're bound to win.

MITA: Ah yes, there're two of us.

OLD MAN: But there's one of him, that's only one less.

MITA: He could easily be ten less.

OLD MAN: If he was ten less I'd give him some sand.

MITA: And I'd give him a branch.

CLIMANDO: It's important to be one less, too. For instance, the other day Sato fell in love with a butterfly that I'd put in his pocket and as he didn't know how to declare his love he got up on to a chair and started singing about how love tastes like peaches, until the butterfly understood that as it was going to freeze the river would overflow and that it'd be better to fly over to the hospital pavilion where they keep the potatoes and where the atmosphere is sad. But the potatoes that weren't used to living in sad atmospheres grew blue flags. And in the town they made red sunflowers out of the blue flags. And green poppies out of the red sunflowers. And nightingales out of the green poppies.

He is speaking violently.

And bulbs out of the nightingales, and shoes out of the bulbs, and feathers out of the shoes, and beadles out of the feathers, and brooches out of the beadles, and . . .

OLD MAN [*interrupting him*[: Yes, yes, that's fine, but the cops are over there and any minute now they'll be coming to put you in prison. They're only waiting for their chief.

CLIMANDO: Their chief?

OLD MAN: Yes.

CLIMANDO: Aren't I important!

OLD MAN: Not so important as I am.

CLIMANDO: But you're older.

MITA [*pointing to the right*]: Look, one of them's coming already.

CLIMANDO: Is that the chief?

OLD MAN: No.

CLIMANDO: What's he coming for, then?

OLD MAN: He's the one that's going to deal with you until the chief arrives.

CLIMANDO: Chiefs give me the creeps.

MITA: Yes, all they can do is sneak.

CLIMANDO: Why?

MITA: Because when they're at home their wives beat them.

CLIMANDO: Oh, how nasty of them.

Enter the POLICEMAN.

POLICEMAN: Caracatchitcho, caracotchotchitchi, tchootcha, caracatchi.

MITA [*to the* OLD MAN]: What did he say?

OLD MAN: Tcha, tchay, tcho, or something.

MITA: How extraordinary.

OLD MAN: It's incomprehensible.

The POLICEMAN *is furious and says to* MITA *and the* OLD FLUTE PLAYER:

POLICEMAN: Caracashitcho, caracatchotcha, tch, tchoo, tcha, caracatchi.

MITA *and the* OLD MAN *are slightly scared and move away from their friends.*

OLD MAN: He'd like to beat us up.

MITA: He could.

OLD MAN: Oh, he's not very big!

MITA: But he's sure to be very good at spitting.

OLD MAN: Ah!

The indignant POLICEMAN *speaks to them again and finally makes them go out.*

POLICEMAN: Caracashitcho, caracashitcho, tchi, tchoo, tcha, caracatchi.

Then he turns to APAL *and wakes him up. After which he reproaches* CLIMANDO *and* APAL *in cordial tones.*

Lamelee, la meloo, lee, la, lamela salemi, seemee, la melee.

The POLICEMAN *goes out but immediately comes back with a hammock which he lies in. He takes out a book and starts reading.*

CLIMANDO [*to* APAL]: What's going on?

APAL: We've killed.

CLIMANDO: What are you going to do?

APAL: Sleep until they come and get me.

CLIMANDO: Sleep now? And what if the cop starts beating you up just when you least expect it?

APAL: I shan't feel it so much.

CLIMANDO: I don't think you ought to go to sleep now. What for?

APAL: So as not to have to talk . . . so as not to have to hear people talking.

CLIMANDO: Don't I talk properly? D'you want me to recite some poems they taught me when I was little? . . . You never ask me to talk to you about anything in particular. I don't know what you like. Tell me to talk to you about something you like, Apal, I'm very good at talking about hens and staircases, and about grasshoppers, and about tricycles, and about storks, and about fishes and meals. Tell me, Apal, what you'd like me to talk about.

APAL: Nothing.

CLIMANDO: You're cross with me.

APAL: No I'm not.

CLIMANDO: Hm! I know you'd rather talk to the old man; he's had more experience and he can play the flute.

APAL: No I wouldn't.

CLIMANDO: Then you must be tired.

APAL: I've no idea.

CLIMANDO: Well, you must know, because it does matter . . . Oh, I know; you're always sleeping because you're sleepy.

APAL: Yes.

CLIMANDO: Why didn't you say so, before?

APAL: I didn't know it.

CLIMANDO [*speaking slowly and at length*]: Well, if you didn't know it before, how come you realise it now? It's incomprehensible. There must be some sort of order. First people think about what they've got to do, and then they try and do what they've thought about. If they can't do it, then they stop trying, and so they don't do it. But if they can try, then they ought to do their best to do it, to put what they've tried to do into practice, or almost, but if they do their best to put what they've tried to do into practice, or almost, and they can't solve the problem, then that's all there is to it, but if they can, then they do what they have to do without any further beating about the bush, without either thinking about the attempts they've made, or the possibility of anything being certain. But with people who don't try to think, what they attempt comes to nothing. In short, what I'm saying is that there must be some sort of order, we must know why we've said what we *have* said, what we're going to do, and what we *will* do. That's the system I use with the old flute player, and that's why I always win. *He* says I cheat. Me, cheat? That can't be true, can it?

APAL: It can't be true. [APAL *falls asleep.*]

CLIMANDO: My motto is: 'To know what you could have done and what you haven't done.' Everything, absolutely everything, in perfect order. It's not for nothing that we are thinking people. That's why I don't understand why you don't remember what you were going to do now or what you did yesterday. It all comes from a lack of order. A hell of a lack of order. We must have some sort of order, a straight, rational path, we must find the best way to behave. Apal, don't go to sleep!

APAL: I'll do my best.

CLIMANDO: I'll go on. It'll help you to understand if I give you an example. A man was carrying a pitcher of wine, and an old woman sitting by the door of a house belonging to another man from the same village said to him . . . —pay attention to this detail, it gives you the key—'why are you carrying a pitcher of wine when you could have bought four elephants?' And the man replied: 'I didn't buy four elephants because they haven't been invented yet' . . . Do you understand? Apal, don't go to sleep. What's the matter with you?

APAL: I'm sleepy.

CLIMANDO: If you go to sleep I'll get bored. And when I get bored it makes me sad.

APAL: Then I'll make an effort not to go to sleep.

CLIMANDO [dignified]: Don't make an effort on *my* account.

APAL: Right. [APAL *goes to sleep*].

CLIMANDO: I only said that to see what you'd say.

APAL [sitting up]: Ah!

CLIMANDO: Don't you think we'll be bored in prison?

APAL: Haven't thought about it.

CLIMANDO: And what shall we see?

APAL: We'll see that they're soon going to kill us.

CLIMANDO: Are they going to kill us soon?

APAL: Yes.

CLIMANDO: It's because of the man with the banknotes, isn't it?

APAL: Yes.

CLIMANDO: Will they let us ask them to forgive us?

APAL: I don't know.

CLIMANDO: And is it certain that they'll kill us?

APAL: Yes.

CLIMANDO: Well, I'm off, then.

    CLIMANDO *gets on to the tricycle, all set to escape.*

POLICEMAN [*reproachfully*]: Caracatchitcho, caracotchotcho, tcha, tche, tchi, caracatchi.

> CLIMANDO *gets off the tricycle and sits down again by* APAL.

CLIMANDO: Then it *is* true that they'll kill us?

APAL: Yes.

CLIMANDO: Both of us?

APAL: Yes.

CLIMANDO: Isn't one enough?

APAL: No.

CLIMANDO: But *we* only killed one person.

APAL: Yes.

> *Pause.*

CLIMANDO: Well you needn't think I'm so pleased at being killed now.

APAL: It doesn't make any difference.

CLIMANDO: Oh go on! Now of all times! When I was least expecting it.

> *Silence.*

And what do you think about it?

APAL: About what?

CLIMANDO: About them killing us.

APAL: Not much.

CLIMANDO: Apal, I'm sorry about this—for you.

APAL: Thanks.

CLIMANDO: Don't think I'm so terribly sorry about myself— what annoys me is that it should be so sudden. I'm sorrier about it for you, Apal.

APAL: Pooh, don't let it worry you.

CLIMANDO: What would you like me to do for you?

APAL: Let me sleep.

CLIMANDO: Won't you be afraid?

APAL: No.

CLIMANDO: Right, goodbye, have a good rest.

> CLIMANDO *walks round the* POLICEMAN *several times, trying to read the title of his book.* APAL *sleeps. Enter* MITA, *on all fours. She is certainly afraid the* POLICEMAN *might see her.*

100

MITA: Psst!

CLIMANDO: Mita.

    MITA *moves towards* CLIMANDO.

Hide, don't let the cop see you.

MITA: He won't see me, he's reading.

CLIMANDO: Yes, but he reads very quickly.

MITA: I read more quickly than he does.

CLIMANDO: All right, but be careful.

MITA: What are they going to do to you?

    MITA *moves nearer, her head down and keeping as close to the ground as possible.*

CLIMANDO: They're going to put us in prison and then they'll kill us.

MITA [*terrified*]: Kill you?

CLIMANDO: Are you starting again with your superstitions?

MITA: No, Climando. [*Pause.*] Then you must find some way of saving yourself from going to prison.

CLIMANDO: It's very difficult.

MITA: You *are* in a mess.

CLIMANDO [*joyfully*]: I've got very long legs, I could run.

MITA: And what if they don't know you've got long legs?

CLIMANDO: I'll tell them.

MITA: And what if they catch you?

CLIMANDO: I hadn't thought of that. It'd be better if I told them some stories.

MITA: Yes, do, you know some lovely tales.

CLIMANDO: That's it; if they catch me I'll tell them a story.

MITA [*enthusiastically*]: The one about the little donkey that went to Texas and pricked up his ears and made them V-shaped, you tell it so well.

CLIMANDO: Oh no, not that one, they'll say it's politics.

MITA [*trying to think*]: Right, then the story about the horse that fell in love with a telescope, thinking it was a lamb.

CLIMANDO: They won't like that story either, they'll say they don't understand, and then they'll want to burn me alive.

MITA: Yes, that's the trouble with telling things people don't understand.

CLIMANDO: Which one d'you think I ought to tell?

MITA: Tell them you love me.

CLIMANDO: Oh yes! Isn't that nice! . . . But for that I'd need to have you with me, so that when I say: 'I love her knees, they're so white and smooth and big,' I can lift up your skirts and show them to them. And so that when I say: 'She has a sweet little blond moustache that I like very much,' I can show them. And when I say that your eyes are green, and as pretty as the tricycle was before it got so ugly, and that your hair is as blond as fresh bread, I'll need you to be there, so that we can see each other and they can see us. And when I tell them . . . [*he moves closer to* MITA] that I kiss you . . .

POLICEMAN [*interupting them*]: Caracatchitchipiripipipipi. *The* POLICEMAN *speaks without raising his head from his book.*

CLIMANDO: What did he say?

MITA: Caracatchitcha paripipipi.

CLIMANDO: No no, he said caratchisho piripipipe.

MITA: Don't contradict me.

CLIMANDO: I'm not contradicting you. What I heard was caracatchiche piripipipe.

MITA: How contrary you are, you have a mania for arguing.

POLICEMAN: Caracatchitchi, piripipipi.

CLIMANDO *goes up to the* POLICEMAN *timidly.*

CLIMANDO: Did you say caracatchishe piripipipe or caracatchitcha parapipipi?

The POLICEMAN *clicks his tongue four times and doesn't listen to* CLIMANDO. CLIMANDO, *wanting to get into the* POLICEMAN'S *good books, takes various objects out of the box tricycle, and presents them to him humbly; a spanner, a cardboard box, two glass tubes, a chipped chamber pot, some pages from a calendar, and a tin of sardines. The* POLICEMAN *brushes him away with the back of his hand, without stopping reading for a single moment.*

[*To* MITA]: He must have seen you're with me. Try and hide—and specially the bottom of your skirt. I'll walk about a bit, to hide you.

CLIMANDO *walks up and down.*

CLIMANDO: The duties of a tricycle driver. . . .

> CLIMANDO *is speaking in a sing-song voice like a school-boy.*

are . . . definitions . . . classes . . . relations with bachelors . . . [*to* MITA] I can't go on like that because he'll find out that I don't know it.

MITA: Say 'no news' several times, then.

CLIMANDO [*walking up and down*]: No news, no news, no news.

> CLIMANDO *continues to walk up and down, saying* 'no news' *over and over again.*

MITA [*softly*]: Listen, Climando, say it in different ways, or he'll notice that you keep saying the same thing.

CLIMANDO [*saying it in a different tone of voice each time*]: No news, no news. [CLIMANDO *repeats it several times.*] It's all very well, but it makes me tired.

MITA: You mustn't get tired, though.

CLIMANDO: But I'm going to die soon.

MITA: So you think that entitles you to do whatever comes into your head?

CLIMANDO: That'd be the last straw.

MITA: You can't do it, I tell you. I'm going to die, too, and so's Apal, and the old flute player, but that doesn't mean that *we* do what we like.

CLIMANDO: Well I never.

MITA: Do you think, by any chance, that it gives you any right to know the date?

CLIMANDO [*terrified*]: I don't know.

MITA: It's just that someone's done you a favour.

CLIMANDO: I didn't realise.

MITA: And anyway you'll die painlessly, without any trouble, like almost everyone dies.

CLIMANDO: But if they're going to kill me they'll hurt me.

MITA: Not much. Because it's true they'll hurt you, but by the time you feel it you'll be dead.

CLIMANDO: That's fine.

MITA: Wonderful.

CLIMANDO: And what then?

MITA: Then you'll go to heaven.

CLIMANDO [*tenderly*]: If it exists . . . I'll go to heaven with the lambs and with the buses, and with the little donkeys that prick up their ears and make them V-shaped, and with the men who drive tricycles, and with the kids in the park, and old men who play the flute and the violin, and with the leaves on the trees.

MITA [*interrupting him*]: I shall go, too.

CLIMANDO: Yes, and Apal.

MITA: Apal? Not Apal. He knows too much.

CLIMANDO: But he's good. And he sleeps all day long so that no one should realise that he knows so many things.

MITA: But he won't sleep in heaven. That'd be a fine thing! You must realise that he'll be taking someone else's place.

CLIMANDO: Tell me, Mita—where shall we pee in heaven?

MITA: People don't pee in heaven.

CLIMANDO: Oh I *am* sorry.

MITA: You'll get used to it.

CLIMANDO [*enthusiastically*]: Mita, you're so intelligent, you know everything.

MITA: Of course I do.

CLIMANDO: And what'll I do in heaven without you?

MITA: Don't worry, you won't be so badly off. It'll be worse for me, I shan't see your pretty boots any more.

CLIMANDO: If you like, Mita, I'll let you have my turn and they can kill you instead of me.

MITA: What *do* you think? That the cops are idiots and won't notice?

CLIMANDO: It's quite simple, you dress up in my clothes and when they say: 'Climando, we're going to kill you,' you say 'Present.'

MITA: But I can't tell a lie. Because if you want to go to heaven you mustn't lie.

CLIMANDO: We nearly made a terrible mistake!

MITA: You realise how I have to take care of all the details?

CLIMANDO: Yes.

MITA: If I hadn't realised I'd have been in hell in no time.

CLIMANDO [*horrified*]: Don't say that word: if I were to repeat it I'd get myself into terrible trouble.

MITA: It's not that word, it's crust. Have you forgotten it already?

CLIMANDO: Yes.

MITA: You must remember—I say it several times at the end of every month, to make up for your not wanting to say it.

CLIMANDO: Have you said it this month yet?

MITA: No.

CLIMANDO: Well, you're just saying it.

MITA: Crust, crust, crust: three times are enough.

CLIMANDO: How can we know? I once heard someone say that we ought to wear cups on our head to overcome the force of gravity.

MITA: Yes, that gives us a clue, but I insist on telling you that three times are enough.

CLIMANDO: You're always right.

MITA: Because you never know how to argue.

CLIMANDO: That's true enough. Tell me, what are you going to do when I'm dead?

MITA: Not see you any more.

CLIMANDO: I want you to wear mourning for me. All dressed in black, with a black band as well, on your sleeve.

MITA: No, mourning makes me want to giggle.

CLIMANDO: Aren't you brave! Even braver than the legionnaires who laugh at death. You even laugh at mourning.

MITA: What I *can* do, if you like, is always eat shrimps.

CLIMANDO: You'd rather eat a sardine than shrimps all the time.

MITA: You always criticise me because I eat so little.

CLIMANDO: No, Mita, I want to do what you'd like . . . specially when I think that it won't be long before I'm happy in heaven with the sheep and the little donkeys.

MITA: I want to do a lot for you, too.

CLIMANDO: Then it'd be better not to do anything at all, because that way we won't have to put ourselves out.

MITA: Don't we love each other! Don't we understand each other!

CLIMANDO [*amorously*]: Yes.

Enter the OLD FLUTE PLAYER, *hanging his head so as not to be seen.*

OLD MAN: The chief's arrived; he's just over there.

MITA: Tell Apal, then; he ought to know.

CLIMANDO: Apal would rather sleep.

OLD MAN: They say they're going to kill you; I'm so glad.

MITA: So'm I.

CLIMANDO: Me too.

OLD MAN: But you oughtn't to be glad. Just imagine how amusing it's going to be for you!

CLIMANDO: You're the one who oughtn't to be pleased. I don't think it'll be so amusing for you, either.

OLD MAN: I'm pleased because then I shan't argue with you any more and you won't win any more.

MITA: That's an important reason.

CLIMANDO: Is that all?

MITA: Come on, tell the truth, don't be ashamed of it—say that you do love him, really.

OLD MAN [*very much ashamed*]: Well, only a little bit, only a very little bit. That much. [*He points to his nail.*]

MITA [*to* CLIMANDO]: And what about you?

CLIMANDO: That much too.

OLD MAN: I'll leave you the flute, if you like, so you can die to music. [*He gives him his flute.*]

CLIMANDO [*taking it*]: Right.

OLD MAN: It won't disgust you?

CLIMANDO: No, because I wear boots specially for that.

OLD MAN: But what you need is a fur coat for that.

CLIMANDO: But I've got a couple of pairs of pliers for that.

OLD MAN: But you need a couple of cauliflowers for that.

CLIMANDO: But I've got three toothpicks for that.

OLD MAN: But you need three raincoats for that.

CLIMANDO: But I've got four typewriters for that.

OLD MAN: But you need four pairs of cotton pyjamas for that.

CLIMANDO: But I've got five socks for that.

All these last speeches overlap.

OLD MAN: But you need ten ostriches for that.

CLIMANDO [*to* MITA]: Tell him that I can't have five socks because socks come in pairs.

MITA [*talking into the old man's ear*]: Tell him it's not true he can't have five socks because socks come in pairs.

OLD MAN [*very pleased*]: It's not true, it's not true, it's not true. You can't have five socks because socks come in pairs; I've won.

CLIMANDO: You cheated.

OLD MAN: No I didn't.

Enter the POLICE CHIEF.

POLICEMAN [*saluting his superior*]: Cara.

The two policemen talk to each other.

CLIMANDO: Get up, Apal, they've come for us.

APAL: I'm coming.

CLIMANDO: As they're going to kill me, Mita, I'll give you my boots.

CLIMANDO *takes off his boots; his feet are bare. He gives the boots to* MITA.

MITA [*putting them on*]: Pity they've got holes in them.

CLIMANDO [*to the* OLD MAN]: And I leave you the tricycle.

OLD MAN [*enthusiastically*]: The tricycle! Can I stroke the kids?

CLIMANDO: Yes.

OLD MAN: And will you leave me the bells, too?

CLIMANDO: Yes.

OLD MAN: And the pages from the calendar?

CLIMANDO: Yes.

OLD MAN: And the pot?

CLIMANDO: Yes.

OLD MAN: And the pliers?

CLIMANDO: Yes.

OLD MAN: And the wire?

CLIMANDO: Yes. But don't ask me for any more or you'll get to be like a tortoise.

OLD MAN: That's true.

107

MITA [*to* APAL]: Are they going to kill you, too?

APAL: Looks like it.

MITA: Give me your jacket, then.

APAL: My jacket?

MITA: Yes.

APAL: I'll be cold. It's winter.

MITA: Pooh, you've so little time left to live.

APAL: All right.

He takes off his jacket and gives it to MITA. THE POLICE-MEN *stop talking. The first* POLICEMAN *goes over to* MITA *and the* OLD MAN *and separates them from their friends by yelling*:

POLICEMAN: Caracatchisho, piripipipi.

The POLICE CHIEF *handcuffs* APAL *and* CLIMANDO. APAL, *without his jacket, is shivering with cold.* CLIMANDO *moves his naked toes to try and warm them. The* OLD FLUTE PLAYER *looks at the tricycle.* MITA *looks at the boots and the jacket.*

Atara!

The POLICEMAN *pushes* APAL *and* CLIMANDO *to get them started. With the* CHIEF *and the* POLICEMAN *on either side of them they all four go off.* MITA *and the* OLD MAN *are left on the stage.* MITA *puts on* APAL'S *jacket. The* OLD FLUTE PLAYER, *helped by* MITA, *gets into the box part of the tricycle.* MITA *rides it, the* OLD MAN *rings the bells, the tricycle crosses the stage and goes off.*

CURTAIN

PICNIC ON THE BATTLEFIELD

CHARACTERS

ZAPO	*A soldier*
MONSIEUR TÉPAN	*The soldier's father*
MADAME TÉPAN	*The soldier's mother*
ZÉPO	*An enemy soldier*
FIRST STRETCHER BEARER	
SECOND STRETCHER BEARER	

Picnic on the Battlefield *premièred on April 25, 1959, in Paris, at the Théâtre de Lutèce, directed by Jean-Marie Serreau.*

PICNIC ON THE BATTLEFIELD

*A battlefield. The stage is covered with barbed wire and
sandbags.
The battle is at its height. Rifle shots, exploding bombs
and machine guns can be heard.*
ZAPO *is alone on the stage, flat on his stomach, hidden
among the sandbags. He is very frightened. The sound of
the fighting stops. Silence.*
ZAPO *takes a ball of wool and some needles out of a
canvas workbag and starts knitting a pullover, which is
already quite far advanced. The field telephone, which is
by his side, suddenly starts ringing.*

ZAPO: Hallo, hallo ... yes, Captain ... yes, I'm the sentry of
sector 47 . . . Nothing new, Captain . . . Excuse me,
Captain, but when's the fighting going to start again?
And what am I supposed to do with the hand-grenades?
Do I chuck them in front of me or behind me? ... Don't
get me wrong, I didn't mean to annoy you ... Captain, I
really feel terribly lonely, couldn't you send me someone
to keep me company? ... Even if it's only a nanny-goat?
[*The Captain is obviously severely reprimanding him.*]
Whatever you say, Captain, whatever you say.

> ZAPO *hangs up. He mutters to himself. Silence. Enter*
> MONSIEUR *and* MADAME TÉPAN, *carrying baskets as if
> they are going to a picnic. They address their son, who
> has his back turned and doesn't see them come in.*

MONS. T. [*ceremoniously*]: Stand up, my son, and kiss your
mother on the brow. [ZAPO, *surprised, gets up and kisses
his mother very respectfully on the forehead. He is about
to speak, but his father doesn't give him a chance.*] And
now, kiss *me.*

ZAPO: But, dear Father and dear Mother, how did you dare to come all this way, to such a dangerous place? You must leave at once.

MONS. T.: So you think you've got something to teach your father about war and danger, do you? All this is just a game to me. How many times—to take the first example that comes to mind—have I got off an underground train while it was still moving.

MME. T.: We thought you must be bored, so we came to pay you a little visit. This war must be a bit tedious, after all.

ZAPO: It all depends.

MONS. T.: I know exactly what happens. To start with you're attracted by the novelty of it all. It's fun to kill people, and throw hand-grenades about, and wear uniforms—you feel smart, but in the end you get bored stiff. You'd have found it much more interesting in my day. Wars were much more lively, much more highly coloured. And then, the best thing was that there were horses, plenty of horses. It was a real pleasure; if the Captain ordered us to attack, there we all were immediately, on horseback, in our red uniforms. It was a sight to be seen. And then there were the charges at the gallop, sword in hand, and suddenly you found yourself face to face with the enemy, and he was equal to the occasion too—with his horses—there were always horses, lots of horses, with their well-rounded rumps—in his highly-polished boots, and his green uniform.

MME. T.: No no, the enemy uniform wasn't green. It was blue. I remember distinctly that it was blue.

MONS. T.: I tell you it was green.

MME. T.: When I was little, how many times did I go out on to the balcony to watch the battle and say to the neighbour's little boy: 'I bet you a gum-drop the blues win.' And the blues were our enemies.

MONS. T.: Oh well, you must be right, then.

MME. T.: I've always liked battles. As a child I always said

112

that when I grew up I wanted to be a Colonel of dragoons. But my mother wouldn't hear of it, you know how she will stick to her principles at all costs.

MONS. T.: Your mother's just a half-wit.

ZAPO: I'm sorry, but you really must go. You can't come into a war unless you're a soldier.

MONS. T.: I don't give a damn, we came here to have a picnic with you in the country and to enjoy our Sunday.

MME. T.: And I've prepared an excellent meal, too. Sausage, hard-boiled eggs—you know how you like them!—ham sandwiches, red wine, salad, and cakes.

ZAPO: All right, let's have it your way. But if the Captain comes he'll be absolutely furious. Because he isn't at all keen on us having visits when we're at the front. He never stops telling us: 'Discipline and hand-grenades are what's wanted in a war, not visits.'

MONS. T.: Don't worry, I'll have a few words to say to your Captain.

ZAPO: And what if we have to start fighting again?

MONS. T.: You needn't think that'll frighten me, it won't be the first fighting I've seen. Now if only it was battles on horseback! Times have changed, you can't understand. [*Pause.*] We came by motor bike. No one said a word to us.

ZAPO: They must have thought you were the referees.

MONS. T.: We had enough trouble getting through, though. What with all the tanks and jeeps.

MME. T.: And do you remember the bottle-neck that cannon caused, just when we got here?

MONS. T.: You mustn't be surprised at anything in wartime, everyone knows that.

MME. T.: Good, let's start our meal.

MONS. T.: You're quite right, I feel as hungry as a hunter. It's the smell of gunpowder.

MME. T.: We'll sit on the rug while we're eating.

ZAPO: Can I bring my rifle with me?

MME. T.: You leave your rifle alone. It's not good manners to bring your rifle to table with you. [*Pause.*] But you're

113

absolutely filthy, my boy. How on earth did you get into such a state? Let's have a look at your hands.

ZAPO [*ashamed, holding out his hands*]: I had to crawl about on the ground during the manoeuvres.

MME. T.: And what about your ears?

ZAPO: I washed them this morning.

MME. T.: Well that's all right, then. And your teeth? [*He shows them.*] Very good. Who's going to give her little boy a great big kiss for cleaning his teeth so nicely? [*To her husband*] Well, go on, kiss your son for cleaning his teeth so nicely. [M. TÉPAN *kisses his son.*] Because, you know, there's one thing I *will* not have, and that's making fighting a war an excuse for not washing.

ZAPO: Yes, Mother.

They eat.

MONS. T.: Well, my boy, did you make a good score?

ZAPO: When?

MONS. T.: In the last few days, of course.

ZAPO: Where?

MONS. T.: At the moment, since you're fighting a war.

ZAPO: No, nothing much. I didn't make a good score. Hardly ever scored a bull.

MONS. T.: Which are you best at shooting, enemy horses or soldiers?

ZAPO: No, not horses, there aren't any horses any more.

MONS. T.: Well, soldiers then?

ZAPO: Could be.

MONS. T.: Could be? Aren't you sure?

ZAPO: Well you see . . . I shoot without taking aim, [*pause*] and at the same time I say a Pater Noster for the chap I've shot.

MONS. T.: You must be braver than that. Like your father.

MME. T.: I'm going to put a record on.

She puts a record on the gramophone—a pasodoble. All three are sitting on the ground, listening.

MONS. T.: That really *is* music. Yes indeed, olé!

The music continues. Enter an enemy soldier: ZÉPO. He is dressed like ZAPO. The only difference is the colour of

their uniforms. ZÉPO *is in green and* ZAPO *is in grey.*
ZÉPO *listens to the music openmouthed. He is behind the*
family so they can't see him. The record ends. As he
gets up ZAPO *discoveres* ZÉPO. *Both put their hands up.*
M. *and* MME. TÉPAN *look at them in surprise.*

What's going on?

ZAPO *reacts—he hesitates. Finally, looking as if he's*
made up his mind, he points his rifle at ZÉPO.

ZAPO: Hands up!

ZÉPO *puts his hands up even higher, looking even more*
terrified. ZAPO *doesn't know what to do. Suddenly he*
goes quickly over to ZÉPO *and touches him gently on the*
shoulder, like a child playing a game of 'tag'.

Got you! [*To his father, very pleased.*] There we are! A
prisoner!

MONS. T.: Fine. And now what're you going to do with him?

ZAPO: I don't know, but, well, could be—they might make
me a corporal.

MONS. T.: In the meantime you'd better tie him up.

ZAPO: Tie him up? Why?

MONS. T.: Prisoners always get tied up!

ZAPO: How?

MONS. T.: Tie up his hands.

MME. T.: Yes, there's no doubt about that, you must tie up
his hands, I've always seen them do that.

ZAPO: Right. [*To the prisoner.*] Put your hands together, if
you please.

ZÉPO: Don't hurt me too much.

ZAPO: I won't.

ZÉPO: Ow! You're hurting me.

MONS. T.: Now now, don't maltreat your prisoner.

MME. T.: Is that the way I brought you up? How many times
have I told you that we must be considerate to our fellow-
men?

ZAPO: I didn't do it on purpose. [*To* ZÉPO.] And like that,
does it hurt?

ZÉPO: No, it's all right like that.

115

MONS. T.: Tell him straight out, say what you mean, don't mind us.

ZÉPO: It's all right like that.

MONS. T.: Now his feet.

ZAPO: His feet as well, whatever next?

MONS. T.: Didn't they teach you the rules?

ZAPO: Yes.

MONS. T.: Well then!

ZAPO [*very politely, to* ZÉPO]: Would you be good enough to sit on the ground, please?

ZÉPO: Yes, but don't hurt me.

MME. T.: You'll see, he'll take a dislike to you.

ZAPO: No he won't, no he won't. I'm not hurting you, am I?

ZÉPO: No, that's perfect.

ZAPO: Papa, why don't you take a photo of the prisoner on the ground and me with my foot on his stomach?

MONS. T.: Oh yes, that'd look good.

ZÉPO: Oh no, not that!

MME. T.: Say yes, don't be obstinate.

ZÉPO: No. I said no, and no it is.

MME. T.: But just a little teeny weeny photo, what harm could that do you? And we could put it in the dining room, next to the life-saving certificate my husband won thirteen years ago.

ZÉPO: No—you won't shift me.

ZAPO: But why won't you let us?

ZÉPO: I'm engaged. And if she sees the photo one day, she'll say I don't know how to fight a war properly.

ZAPO: No she won't, all you'll need to say is that it isn't you, it's a panther.

MME. T.: Come on, do say yes.

ZÉPO: All right then. But only to please you.

ZAPO: Lie down flat.

> ZÉPO *lies down.* ZAPO *puts a foot on his stomach and grabs his rifle with a martial air.*

MME. T.: Stick your chest out a bit further.

ZAPO: Like this?

MME. T.: Yes, like that, and don't breathe.

MONS. T.: Try and look like a hero.

ZAPO: What d'you mean, like a hero?

MONS. T.: It's quite simple; try and look like the butcher does when he's boasting about his successes with the girls.

ZAPO: Like this?

MONS. T.: Yes, like that.

MME. T.: The most important thing is to puff your chest out and not breathe.

ZÉPO: Have you nearly finished?

MONS. T.: Just be patient a moment. One . . . two . . . three.

ZAPO: I hope I'll come out well.

MME. T.: Yes, you looked very martial.

MONS. T.: You were fine.

MME. T.: It makes me want to have my photo taken with you.

MONS. T.: Now there's a good idea.

ZAPO: Right. I'll take it if you like.

MME. T.: Give me your helmet to make me look like a soldier.

ZÉPO: I don't want any more photos. Even one's far too many.

ZAPO: Don't take it like that. After all, what harm can it do you?

ZÉPO: It's my last word.

MONS. T. [*to his wife*]: Don't press the point, prisoners are always very sensitive. If we go on he'll get cross and spoil our fun.

ZAPO: Right, what're we going to do with him, then?

MME. T.: We could invite him to lunch. What do you say?

MONS. T.: I don't see why not.

ZAPO [*to* ZÉPO]: Well, will you have lunch with us, then?

ZÉPO: Er . . .

MONS. T.: We brought a good bottle with us.

ZÉPO: Oh well, all right then.

MME. T.: Make yourself at home, don't be afraid to ask for anything you want.

ZÉPO: All right.

MONS. T.: And what about you, did you make a good score?

ZÉPO: When?

MONS. T.: In the last few days, of course.

ZÉPO: Where?

MONS. T.: At the moment, since you're fighting a war.

ZÉPO: No, nothing much. I didn't make a good score, hardly ever scored a bull.

MONS. T.: Which are you best at shooting? Enemy horses or soldiers?

ZÉPO: No, not horses, there aren't any horses any more.

MONS. T.: Well, soldiers then?

ZÉPO: Could be.

MONS. T.: Could be? Aren't you sure?

ZÉPO: Well you see . . . I shoot without taking aim [*pause*], and at the same time I say an Ave Maria for the chap I've shot.

ZAPO: An Ave Maria? I'd have thought you'd have said a Pater Noster.

ZÉPO: No, always an Ave Maria. [*Pause.*] It's shorter.

MONS. T.: Come come, my dear fellow, you must be brave.

MME. T. [*to* ZÉPO]: We can untie you if you like.

ZÉPO: No, don't bother, it doesn't matter.

MONS. T.: Don't start getting stand-offish with us now. If you'd like us to untie you, say so.

MME. T.: Make yourself comfortable.

ZÉPO: Well, if that's how you feel, you can untie my feet, but it's only to please you.

MONS. T.: Zapo, untie him.

    ZAPO *unties him.*

MME. T.: Well, do you feel better?

ZÉPO: Yes, of course. I really am putting you to a lot of inconvenience.

MONS. T.: Not at all, just make yourself at home. And if you'd like us to untie your hands you only have to say so.

ZÉPO: No, not my hands, I don't want to impose upon you.

MONS. T: No no, my dear chap, no no. I tell you, it's no trouble at all.

ZÉPO: Right . . . Well then, untie my hands too. But only for lunch, eh? I don't want you to think that you give me an inch and I take an ell.

MONS. T.: Untie his hands, son.

MME. T.: Well, since our distinguished prisoner is so charming, we're going to have a marvellous day in the country.

ZÉPO: Don't call me your distinguished prisoner, just call me your prisoner.

MME. T.: Won't that embarrass you?

ZÉPO: No no, not at all.

MONS. T.: Well, I must say you're modest.

Noise of aeroplanes.

ZAPO: Aeroplanes. They're sure to be coming to bomb us.

ZAPO *and* ZÉPO *throw themselves on the sandbags and hide.*

[*To his parents*]:Take cover. The bombs will fall on you.

The noise of the aeroplanes overpowers all the other noises. Bombs immediately start to fall. Shells explode very near the stage but not on it. A deafening noise.

ZAPO *and* ZÉPO *are cowering down between the sandbags.* M. TÉPAN *goes on talking calmly to his wife, and she answers in the same unruffled way. We can't hear what they are saying because of the bombing.* MME. TÉPAN *goes over to one of the baskets and takes an umbrella out of it. She opens it.* M. *and* MME. TÉPAN *shelter under it as if it were raining. They are standing up. They shift rhythmically from one foot to the other and talk about their personal affairs.*

The bombing continues.

Finally the aeroplanes go away. Silence.

M. TÉPAN *stretches an arm outside the umbrella to make sure that nothing more is falling from the heavens.*

MONS. T. [*to his wife*]: You can shut your umbrella.

MME. TÉPAN *does so. They both go over to their son and tap him lightly on the behind with the umbrella.*

Come on, out you come. The bombing's over.

ZAPO *and* ZÉPO *come out of their hiding place.*

ZAPO: Didn't you get hit?

MONS. T.: What d'you think could happen to your father? [*Proudly.*] Little bombs like that! Don't make me laugh!

Enter, left, two RED CROSS SOLDIERS. *They are carrying a stretcher.*

1st STRETCHER BEARER: Any dead here?

ZAPO: No, no one around these parts.

1st STRETCHER BEARER: Are you sure you've looked properly?

ZAPO: Sure.

1st STRETCHER BEARER: And there isn't a single person dead?

ZAPO: I've already told you there isn't.

1st STRETCHER BEARER: No one wounded, even?

ZAPO: Not even that.

2nd STRETCHER BEARER [*to the* 1st S. B.]: Well, now we're in a mess! [*To* ZAPO *persuasively.*] Just look again, search everywhere, and see if you can't find us a stiff.

1st STRETCHER BEARER: Don't keep on about it, they've told you quite clearly there aren't any.

2nd STRETCHER BEARER: What a lousy trick!

ZAPO: I'm terribly sorry. I promise you I didn't do it on purpose.

2nd STRETCHER BEARER: That's what they all say. That no one's dead and that they didn't do it on purpose.

1st STRETCHER BEARER: Oh, let the chap alone!

MONS. T. [*obligingly*]: We should be only too pleased to help you. At your service.

2nd STRETCHER BEARER: Well, really, if things go on like this I don't know what the Captain will say to us.

MONS. T.: But what's it all about?

2nd STRETCHER BEARER: Quite simply that the others' wrists are aching with carting so many corpses and wounded men about, and that we haven't found any yet. And it's not because we haven't looked!

MONS. T.: Well yes, that really is annoying. [*To* ZAPO.] Are you quite sure no one's dead?

ZAPO: Obviously, Papa.

MONS. T.: Have you looked under all the sandbags?

ZAPO: Yes, Papa.

MONS. T. [*angrily*]: Well then, you might as well say straight out that you don't want to lift a finger to help these gentlemen, when they're so nice, too!

1st STRETCHER BEARER: Don't be angry with him. Let him be. We must just hope we'll have more luck in another trench and that all the lot'll be dead.

MONS. T.: I should be delighted.

MME. T.: Me too. There's nothing I like more than people who put their hearts into their work.

MONS. T. [*indignantly, addressing his remarks to the wings*]: Then is no one going to do anything for these gentlemen?

ZAPO: If it only rested with me, it'd already be done.

ZÉPO: I can say the same.

MONS. T.: But look here, is neither of you even wounded?

ZAPO [*ashamed*]: No, not me.

MONS. T. [*to* ZÉPO]: What about you?

ZÉPO [*ashamed*]: Me neither. I never have any luck.

MME. T. [*pleased*]: Now I remember! This morning, when I was peeling the onions, I cut my finger. Will that do you?

MONS. T.: Of course it will! [*Enthusiastically.*] They'll take you off at once!

1st STRETCHER BEARER: No, that won't work. With ladies it doesn't work.

MONS. T.: We're no further advanced, then.

1st STRETCHER BEARER: Never mind.

2nd STRETCHER BEARER: We may be able to make up for it in the other trenches.

They start to go off.

MONS. T.: Don't worry! If we find a dead man we'll keep him for you! No fear of us giving him to anyone else!

2nd STRETCHER BEARER: Thank you very much, sir.

MONS. T.: Quite all right, old chap, think nothing of it.

The two STRETCHER BEARERS *say goodbye. All four answer them. The* STRETCHER BEARERS *go out.*

MMT. T.: That's what's so pleasant about spending a Sunday in the country. You always meet such nice people. [*Pause.*] But why are you enemies?

ZÉPO: I don't know, I'm not very well educated.

MME. T.: Was it by birth, or did you become enemies afterwards?

ZÉPO: I don't know, I don't know anything about it.

MONS. T. Well then, how did you come to be in the war?

ZÉPO: One day, at home, I was just mending my mother's iron, a man came and asked me: 'Are you Zépo?' 'Yes.' 'Right, you must come to the war.' And so I asked him: 'But what war?' and he said: 'Don't you read the papers then? You're just a peasant!' I told him I did read the papers but not the war bits. . . .

ZAPO: Just how it was with me—exactly how it was with me.

MONS. T.: Yes, they came to fetch you too.

MME. T.: No, it wasn't quite the same; that day you weren't mending an iron, you were mending the car.

MONS. T.: I was talking about the rest of it. [To ZÉPO.] Go on, what happened then?

ZÉPO: Then I told him I had a fiancée and that if I didn't take her to the pictures on Sundays she wouldn't like it. He said that that wasn't the least bit important.

ZAPO: Just how it was with me—exactly how it was with me.

ZÉPO: And then my father came down and he said I couldn't go to the war because I didn't have a horse.

ZAPO: Just what my father said.

ZÉPO: The man said you didn't need a horse any more, and I asked him if I could take my fiancée with me. He said no. Then I asked whether I could take my aunt with me so that she could make me one of her custards on Thursdays; I'm very fond of them.

MME. T. [realising that she'd forgotten it]: Oh! The custard!

ZÉPO: He said no again.

ZAPO: Same as with me.

ZÉPO: And ever since then I've been alone in the trench nearly all the time.

MME. T.: I think you and your distinguished prisoner might play together this afternoon, as you're so close to each other and so bored.

ZAPO: Oh no, Mother, I'm too afraid, he's an enemy.

MONS. T.: Now now, you mustn't be afraid.

ZAPO: If you only knew what the General was saying about the enemy!

MME. T.: What did he say?

ZAPO: He said the enemy are very nasty people. When they take prisoners they put little stones in their shoes so that it hurts them to walk.

MME. T.: How awful! What barbarians!

MONS. T. [*indignantly, to* ZÉPO]: And aren't you ashamed to belong to an army of criminals?

ZÉPO: I haven't done anything. I don't do anybody any harm.

MME. T.: He was trying to take us in, pretending to be such a little saint!

MONS. T.: We oughtn't to have untied him. You never know, we only need to turn our backs and he'll be putting a stone in our shoes.

ZÉPO: Don't be so nasty to me.

MONS. T.: What d'you think we *should* be, then? I'm indignant. I know what I'll do. I'll go and find the Captain and ask him to let me fight in the war.

ZAPO: He won't let you, you're too old.

MONS. T.: Then I'll buy myself a horse and a sword and come and fight on my own account.

MME. T.: Bravo! If I were a man I'd do the same.

ZÉPO: Don't be like that with me, Madame. Anyway I'll tell you something—our General told us the same thing about you.

MME. T.: How could he dare tell such a lie!

ZAPO: No—but the same thing really?

ZÉPO: Yes, the same thing.

MONS. T.: Perhaps it was the same man who talked to you both?

MME. T.: Well if it was the same man he might at least have said something different. That's a fine thing—saying the same thing to everyone!

MONS. T. [*to* ZÉPO, *in a different tone of voice*]: Another little drink?

MME. T.: I hope you liked our lunch?

MONS. T.: In any case, it was better than last Sunday.

ZÉPO: What happened?

MONS. T.: Well, we went to the country and we put the food on the rug. While we'd got our backs turned a cow ate up all our lunch, and the napkins as well.

ZÉPO: What a greedy cow!

MONS. T.: Yes, but afterwards, to get our own back, we ate the cow.

They laugh.

ZAPO [*to* ZÉPO]: They couldn't have been very hungry after that!

MONS. T.: Cheers! [*They all drink.*]

MME. T. [*to* ZÉPO]: And what do you do to amuse yourself in the trench?

ZÉPO: I spend my time making flowers out of rags, to amuse myself. I get terribly bored.

MME. T.: And what do you do with the flowers?

ZÉPO: At the beginning I used to send them to my fiancée, but one day she told me that the greenhouse and the cellar were already full of them and that she didn't know what to do with them any more, and she asked me, if I didn't mind, to send her something else.

MME. T.: And what did you do?

ZÉPO: I tried to learn to make something else, but I couldn't. So I go on making rag flowers to pass the time.

MME. T.: Do you throw them away afterwards, then?

ZÉPO: No, I've found a way to use them now. I give one flower for each pal who dies. That way I know that even if I make an awful lot there'll never be enough.

MONS. T.: That's a good solution you've hit on.

ZÉPO [*shyly*]: Yes.

ZAPO: Well, what I do is knit, so as not to get bored.

MME. T.: But tell me, are all the soldiers as bored as you?

ZÉPO: It all depends on what they do to amuse themselves.

ZAPO: It's the same on our side.

MONS. T.: Then let's stop the war.

ZÉPO: How?

MONS. T.: It's very simple.[*To* ZAPO.]You just tell your pals
that the enemy soldiers don't want to fight a war, and you
[*to* ZÉPO] say the same to your comrades. And then everyone goes home.

ZAPO: Marvellous!

MME. T.: And then you'll be able to finish mending the iron.

ZAPO: How is it that no one thought of such a good idea
before?

MME. T.: Your father is the only one who's capable of thinking up such ideas; don't forget he's a former student of the
Ecole Normale, *and* a philatelist.

ZÉPO: But what will the sergeant-majors and corporals
do?

MONS. T.: We'll give them some guitars and castanets to keep
them quiet!

ZÉPO: Very good idea.

MONS. T.: You see how easy it is. Everything's fixed.

ZÉPO: We shall have a tremendous success.

ZAPO: My pals will be terribly pleased.

MME. T.: What d'you say to putting on the pasodoble we
were playing just now, to celebrate?

ZÉPO: Perfect.

ZAPO: Yes, put the record on, Mother.

> MME. TÉPAN *puts a record on. She turns the handle. She
> waits. Nothing can be heard.*

MONS. T.: I can't hear a thing.

MME. T.: Oh, how silly of me! Instead of putting a record on
I put on a beret.

> *She puts the record on. A gay pasodoble is heard.* ZAPO
> *dances with* ZÉPO, *and* MME. TÉPAN *with her husband.
> They are all very gay. The field telephone rings. None of
> the four hears it. They go on dancing busily. The telephone
> rings again. The dance continues.*
> *The battle starts up again with a terrific din of bombs,
> shots and bursts of machine-gun fire. None of the four
> has seen anything and they go on dancing merrily. A burst
> of machine-gun fire mows them all down. They fall to the
> ground, stone dead. A shot must have grazed the gramo-*

phone; the record keeps repeating the same thing, like a
scratched record. The music of the scratched record can
be heard till the end of the play.
The two STRETCHER BEARERS *enter left. They are carrying*
the empty stretcher.

SUDDEN CURTAIN